Olivier Clément

The Other Sun
A Spiritual Autobiography

The Other Sun

A Spiritual Autobiography

Olivier Clément

translated and annotated with an introduction by

Michael Donley

GRACEWING

First published in France as *L'Autre Soleil* 1975
First English edition 2021
by
Gracewing
2 Southern Avenue
Leominster
Herefordshire HR6 0QF
United Kingdom
www.gracewing.co.uk

All rights reserved.
No part of this publication may be reproduced,
stored in a retrieval system, or transmitted in any
form or by any means, electronic, mechanical,
photocopying, recording or otherwise, without the
written permission of the publisher.

© 1975, 2010, 2021 the Literary Estate of Olivier Clément
Original French edition *L'Autre Soleil* © 2010 Desclée de Brouwer
Translation © 2021 Michael Donley

The rights of Michael Donley
to be identified as the translator of this work
have been asserted in accordance with the
Copyright, Designs and Patents Act 1988.

ISBN 978 085244 970 7

Typeset by Word and Page, Chester, UK

Cover design by Bernardita Peña Hurtado

Contents

Translator's Introduction	vii
1. Childhood and Youth	1
2. War, Politics and Culture	43
3. Death and Other Enigmas	69
4. The Temptation of the Far East	97
5. Berdyaev	127
6. Sicut Cervus	139
7. Lossky, Father Sophrony, Evdokimov	159
8. Epilogue	191
Bibliography	197

*For Metropolitan Kallistos (Ware) of Diokleia
my spiritual father*

Translator's Introduction

The Orthodox theologian Olivier Clément is best known in the English-speaking world as the author of *The Roots of Christian Mysticism* and *On Human Being*. Yet these texts represent the tip of the iceberg. In all, he wrote some forty books, as well as countless articles, contributions to other volumes, prefaces and introductions. Many will also know that he was the disciple and close friend of Vladimir Lossky, the eminent patristic theologian. In fact, Clément was instrumental in bringing to publication Lossky's books, all of which— excepting *The Mystical Theology of the Eastern Church*— were published posthumously. The recently published *Théologie dogmatique*—which has now appeared in an English version—is based on the notes that Clément made during Lossky's lectures between 1954 and 1958.

From 1959, for almost fifty years Olivier Clément was also the editor of *Contacts*, the influential French Orthodox journal. Its very title points to an important aspect of his understanding of his faith, namely that it should be characterized by a positive openness. One of his books—one that discusses the life and writings of Vladimir Lossky and Paul Evdokimov—is entitled *Deux passeurs*. Yet, being the first non-Russian continuer of the work of the so-called "Paris School", he himself was a *passeur*—a go-between, a mediator, a conveyor of goods from one context to another. Wherever possible, he sought to build bridges between Orthodox and non-Orthodox, between believers and non-believers, between the venerable, living Tradition and the most advanced post-modernity. As he himself once said, his aim was always to place himself at the frontier between faith and a world that has become secularized, demonstrating the *universality* of Orthodoxy in a way that is faithful to Scripture, the Fathers and Tradition, yet captivatingly fresh rather than merely repetitive, and open to all that is true and authentic. He did not simply quote the Fathers but—to use Florovsky's phrase—had "acquired their mind". One might say that he spoke the language of the Fathers, using the vocabulary of today.

Thus, among recent Orthodox theologians, he was one of those most attentive to contemporary thought, to the doubts, questions and fears of post-modern man. The reasons for this are to some extent explained by his childhood and youth, as is made clear in this autobiography. Another contributory factor was surely the nature of his main employment.

The subject of his first degree was history. He also became, at an exceptionally early age, *agrégé de l'université*.[1] For forty years he taught history—which would have included the history of intellectual thought—at the prestigious Lycée Louis-le-Grand, situated in the Latin Quarter opposite the Sorbonne. For his work there, he received the National Order of Merit. This

---

[1] The *agrégation* is a highly competitive civil-service examination for the public-education system. Each year the number of passes and of available country-wide positions is limited. The qualification admits the successful candidates to the ranks of a category of teachers higher than those who pass through the usual certification process, and allows them to teach in undergraduate *classes préparatoires* and in universities.

Lycée has for centuries been a nursery of France's most famous writers, intellectuals, prelates, philosophers, statesmen, scientists and artists. It offers a sixth-form college curriculum but is also, together with the nearby Lycée Henri IV, home to the oldest and most selective "preparatory classes" in the country. These classes form in effect a post-secondary-level section of the Lycée, their function being to "prepare" students for entry to the elite grandes écoles that train administrative, scientific and business executives for their place as leaders in government or in private enterprise. Entry to the Lycée is itself highly competitive, the strict selection process being based on academic grades and drawing from schools throughout France. The recruitment of teachers is likewise highly selective. This was a teaching post that ensured that Olivier Clément was always in touch with, and receptive to, the concerns of France's most intelligent young people and with the burning questions of the day. "I like listening", reads the opening sentence of the present book, "to people talk about themselves." Since his death, several people have confirmed the truth of this statement, of his readiness to listen to others, of his attentiveness to their individual presence. Most interesting, perhaps, are the testimonies of those acquaintances and friends who have stressed just how their own children were struck by his receptiveness. Typical was the admission of one girl to her father that she had never been taken so seriously by an adult in her entire life.[2]

In France, the timetable and duties of teachers at such lycées are more akin to those of a university lecturer than in the Anglo-Saxon model. Although he

---

[2] "In memoriam", *Contacts, Revue française de l'Orthodoxie*, 228 (2009), 397.

loved his job and believed that history could be viewed in spiritual terms as posing "ultimate questions", this helps explain why from 1962 Clément was able simultaneously for some thirty-five years to be on the staff of the Orthodox Institut Saint-Serge (specializing in moral theology and Church history). He also gave regular lectures at other renowned Parisian institutions such as the Institut supérieur d'études œcuméniques, the Institut Catholique, the École Cathédrale de Paris and the Centre Sèvres, the university-level Jesuit faculty of theology and philosophy.

✥

Olivier Clément was eighty-seven years old when he died in 2009, yet, though reprinted shortly after his death, *L'Autre Soleil* was first published in 1975 when he was only fifty-two. This is not normally an age at which one sets out to write an autobiography. However, this is no normal autobiography, and we will be disappointed if we expect to find in it a detailed account of the author's life, work and activities. The adjective "spiritual" points to the book's main focus. It is less the story of his life than the story of God in his life, the story of how God entered his life. It draws to a close shortly after the account of his baptism.

He wrote it, he said in a radio interview given shortly after its publication, after an episode of serious ill-health, when he understandably felt inclined to take stock of his life. He added that he thought that it might prove to be of some use to others who were searching for the truth.

> Between the ages of forty and fifty certain things are decided. You just carry on as you were, or else you rediscover a deeper truth … It was my own childhood that I found again in writing this

book—writing it like a poem. It had been well and truly lost. In becoming an adult, we adulterate. We adulterate the child we once were, the child's gaze we once had. And yet I have always thought that God's judgment would itself take the form of a child's gaze—that of my own childhood—cast over my life, with astonishment and lucidity.[3]

It is the story of a young Mediterranean pagan who was born in 1921 in Aniane, a village thirty-five kilometres north-west of Montpellier, and who grew up in the dazzling landscape of the Midi, the south of France; the story of how, despite his sense of wonder at the beauty of his surroundings, he suffered from existential angst and a refusal to accept the answers given to his own ultimate questions by his atheist family.

Studying history at Montpellier University, participating in the Resistance during the Second World War (from 1943 to 1945), and flirting with Marxism, he also investigated the myths and religions of the world (especially, long before this became fashionable, those of Asia) in his search for a meaning to life. It was a search which ended in an impasse, for the attractive Hindu sense of unity ultimately leads to nothing but fusion and an impersonal divine, whereas the equally attractive European sense of the uniqueness of each person seemed permanently to be threatened by the danger of fragmentation, isolation and loneliness. Then, after the war, alone in Paris as a young teacher, he was all but overcome by despair and the temptation to commit suicide. The solution was in the end found in Vladimir Lossky's *The Mystical Theology of the Eastern Church*. Not, significantly, in its pages on the Incarna-

[3] Interviewed by Jacques Chancel for *Radioscopie*, his celebrated cultural programme, on Radio France Inter (16 January 1976).

tion or, say, the existence or otherwise of the Deity, but in the chapter on the Trinity. For in the Trinity absolute unity—a unity even more total than that offered by Hinduism—and an equally absolute diversity are harmonized. Seeking the author out and getting to know him, he was eventually baptized into the Orthodox Church (in the parish attended by Lossky) in 1952 at the age of thirty.

Hence the book's main title. For unlike André Gide or Albert Camus,[4] he was ultimately led to see beyond the bright light of the Mediterranean with its sensuous "religion of the sun" and to discover, or rather be found by, "the Other Sun"—Christ, the "Sun of Righteousness" as the Orthodox sing in the main Christmas hymn.[5]

☦

Being a previously unbaptized convert from atheism—rather than from another religion or another Christian denomination (and dissatisfied with it for this or that reason)—Clément effortlessly avoids the trap of understanding Orthodoxy negatively, as something which is characterized as being "against" something else, of being simply what Catholicism or Protestantism is not. This non-aggressive stance is presumably why the late Ecumenical Patriarch Athenagoras, in a

---

[4] Gide's *Les Nourritures terrestres* (*The Fruits of the Earth*) of 1897 and Camus's *Noces* (*Nuptials*) from the 1930s—both set in North Africa—are classic accounts of modern, sensual, Mediterranean paganism.

[5] This phrase, which is also used by Charles Wesley in the hymn become known as "Hark! The herald angels sing", alludes to Malachi's prophecy (4:2) that a Saviour ("the sun of righteousness") would indeed come and would "arise with healing in his wings". On carol sheets the phrase is too often misprinted as "*Son* of righteousness".

play on words, once described him as a "théologien clément". Not surprisingly, among his international friends were to be found not only senior figures in the Orthodox Church, but also Brother Roger, the founder of the Taizé Community, Andrea Riccardi, the founder of the Community of Sant'Egidio, and also Pope John-Paul II. The latter asked him to compose the Meditations for the Via Crucis in the Colosseum in 1998, having been impressed by the calm, reflective and non-polemical way in which—in *Rome autrement*, a book published the previous year and translated later (with a less than faithful title) as *You are Peter*—Clément had taken up the challenge (in *Ut Unum Sint*) for all Christians to explore together the Petrine office.

However, Olivier Clément was not just a theologian or historian but a man of letters, a genuine, creative writer. It is significant that he was not simply a member but president of the French Association of Writers of Faith. French Christians of all denominations, French Jews and Moslems as well as his Orthodox compatriots marvelled at the way in which he put the French language at the service of theology in a manner that was as remarkable from the point of view of style as thought.

His prose, though rich and dense, is elegantly lyrical, and always—despite the occasional use of informal language in an autobiographical text such as this—highly poetic. It is also notoriously difficult to translate. This is especially true of the present text, since its personal nature gives his pen free rein. Indeed, as he said in the interview referred to earlier, he had composed the entire book as if writing a poem. In later years, he did publish two volumes of poetry. He was also a translator of poetry—most notably of T. S. Eliot's *Journey of the Magi*.

Not surprisingly, his theology is never systematic. As he himself insisted, "true theology is not a matter of systems, but a song of glory".[6] "Conceptual, systematic theology", he said elsewhere, "has turned the Word into mere words and made of Christianity nothing but ideological chatter."[7] This helps to explain why he adopts a poetic approach. For the true poet feels no need to engage in an obsessive quest to demonstrate principles; he knows how to use imagery in a way that avoids the partiality offered by concepts. As Ecumenical Patriarch Bartholomew I pointed out in a communiqué delivered at a colloquium held in the Catholic University of Paris in 2009, "Theologians often seek metaphysical answers to contemporary problems, but the truth is that we need more poetry in our theology".[8]

Why is this so? Not simply because the black and white of discursive, speculative, metaphysical prose can become tiresomely abstract as compared with the technicolour and concrete vividness of poetry, but also because a conceptual approach risks descending into atomistic splitting and dispersion. Salvation, on the other hand, is a matter of healing, of integration, of bringing together, of unifying. And this, linguistically, is precisely what poetry itself does.

However, although Clément is not systematic, this does not mean that his writings lack coherence or that they contain no dominant themes. He was himself the first to admit that he generally wrote in response to a request, to a problem or to counter secular arguments

---

[6] O. Clément, "Le sens de la résurrection aujourd'hui", *Revue NUNC*, 7 (Éditions de Corlevour, April 2005), 29.
[7] O. Clément, *Le visage intérieur* (Paris: Stock, 1978), 88.
[8] See *Bulletin*, 336 (March 2009), of the Service Orthodoxe de Presse (Paris).

and the like. Yet isn't this what the Fathers themselves tended to do? A careful reading of his texts reveals that certain favourite themes are indeed discussed time and again. Not, admittedly, in a systematic way, but rather as leitmotivs that re-appear in differing contexts and, like musical variations, in new linguistic permutations. In his book *Olivier Clément: Un passeur*, Franck Damour likens this feature to the use of language in the Church services: "The same themes are taken up on a regular basis, from different perspectives, themes that each time are neither entirely the same nor altogether different, just as in the Liturgy where, with each phrase, everything is already present and yet is always new."[9] This is a pleasing comparison, yet I return to the musical metaphor, not least since it is the one used by Clément himself when describing the style of his two mentors, Lossky and Evdokimov.

If Lossky had to be likened to a musician, he wrote, it would Monteverdi—rigorous, clear and solidly constructed. Evdokimov, on the other hand, he saw as a Debussy—composing a prose that is subtle and pointillist, and at the same time sinuous, twisting and winding like a river that carries in its waters nuggets of gold. Here is how he puts things in the present book: "As for Evdokimov […] his style is full of nuances and reprises that seem disconcerting at first but that turn out to be symphonic. His writings are not that crystal-clear and at times solid 'castle of the soul' that Lossky constructed; it moves like the tide, ebbing and flowing, and yet one eventually realizes that it is making head-

---

[9] F. Damour, *Olivier Clément: Un passeur* (Québec: Éditions Anne Sigier, 2003), 14. I wish to thank Franck Damour for helping me to understand a couple of phrases that were unusually cryptic.

way. With Lossky one learns to think differently; with Evdokimov to feel differently."[10]

This is, in fact, the way *The Other Sun* proceeds. It is less the straightforward account of his conversion than a meditation on spiritually significant events which does not always progress in linear fashion. It too "ebbs and flows", whilst exploring things ever more deeply.

To return to the question of leitmotivs, precisely which ones are they?

We might first mention the one inherited from the Russian religious philosophers: the theme of *divine-humanity*. Clément often stated that, despite the neo-patristic focus of his teacher, Lossky, he gladly acknowledged himself to be the disciple of these religious philosophers as well. He saw no real opposition between the two approaches. A "philosopher" in this special sense of the word might more accurately be described as a creative thinker, rather than a builder of systems or indeed a teacher of the history of the systems other people have built. Clément considered that Russian religious philosophy, though similar to theology, differed in its desire to make sense of and to enlighten culture, society and history with a view to transfiguring them. "To make sense of modernity", as he put it elsewhere, "in the light of Pentecost."[11] To make sense of it, not to adapt to it, nor yet to turn a blind eye to it, but to come to terms with it, to exorcize it and to rise above it.

---

[10] O. Clément, *Orient/Occident. Deux passeurs: Vladimir Lossky, Paul Evdokimov* (Geneva: Labor et Fides, 1985), 10–11.

[11] O. Clément, "Notes autobiographiques", *Contacts*, 228 (2009), 409.

This theme of divine-humanity involves an exploration, in the light of the Incarnation, of what it really means to be human, to be a *person*—a "face", as Clément often puts it.[12] It involves incorporating and answering the criticisms of the so-called "humanists" and atheists (just as the Fathers countered the critics of their own day) and showing to contemporary man as he sleepwalks through life what human beings can be like, if they take Christ as their model. For Christianity is the true humanism, Christ is the true man.

Secondly, Clément's writings are shot through with the dazzling radiance of Pascha, with what he calls—in a sideways dig at Nietzsche—"the gay science of the Resurrection".[13] At the end of *The Roots of Christian Mysticism* he writes, "The spirituality that I have tried to present in this book is a spirituality of resurrection".[14] But this is true of all his writings. In a talk given in 2001, the provocative way in which he took up this theme shows its importance for him. "Is it true", he asks, "that Christ is risen? Or are we liars who content ourselves with singing well?"[15]

As this spiritual autobiography makes clear, Clément was from an early age troubled by death more than is usual, which perhaps explains the vividness of his awareness of Christ's victory over it. Christ compares himself to a doctor; perhaps we should be more specific and claim him to be the original homoeopath, who tramples down death by—death! For Clément,

[12] This is in keeping with the different meanings of the same Greek term, *prosōpon*.
[13] Clément, *Le Visage intérieur*, 83.
[14] O. Clément, *The Roots of Christian Mysticism*, trans. T. Berkeley (London: New City, 1993), 307.
[15] Said during a communication given on the occasion of the first *Journée de l'Orthodoxie en France* (24 May 2001).

this never becomes old news. He often refers to the famous fresco of the Resurrection in the Church of the Holy Saviour in Chora, Constantinople, and also to the mosaic of Christ the Pantocrator, who looks down from one of the domes, and in particular to the inscription it bears: "Jesus Christ, Land of the Living". He even used this as the title of one of his books: *Le Christ, Terre des vivants*. In keeping with Orthodox practice, the fresco does not, of course, depict the rising of Christ himself, but rather Christ in the act of pulling Adam and Eve up out of Hades. Clément delights in speaking of these two icons in the same breath; for, to his constant relief, the land of the dead has become the land of the living.

A third leitmotiv is the insistence on *creativity within Tradition*. To a large extent this derives from the importance that Clément attaches—and which, as he never fails to remind us, God himself attaches—to *human freedom*. This *faithful creativity* found expression in the way he looked to the arts, especially poetry and literature, to speak of God to his contemporaries. It especially found expression in the imaginative way he used his own literary talent, enlightened by the Spirit, to write about the faith. Clément's style enables him to present Christianity in an exciting and sparklingly fresh way. Because of the absence of Christianity in his upbringing, he is able to cut to the quick: Christianity is original and new! It is not in essence a moralizing ideology, but a revolutionary ontological challenge and vocation. In a creative faithfulness, he manages to coin favourite expressions that seize one's attention and capture in a pithy phrase the antinomical truths of the faith. When, for example, referring to the problem of how God can be both transcendent and yet immanent, he writes that this is because he "transcends his own transcendence".[16] Then, linking Isaiah's Suffering Servant with Tabor, he is fond of describing Christ as "disfigured yet transfigured".[17] Of icons, he writes, "An icon avoids all conflict between the figurative and the non-figurative. It is the art of the 'trans-figurative'."[18] For a fourth theme, we can do no better than quote from the communiqué issued by the Assemblée des Évêques Orthodoxes de France, following his death. In it they described him as a *"philokalic* being par excellence", who sought out and attempted to decipher the divine beauty in all places and all people. The Greek metropolitan of France, Emmanuel, in his funeral homily, declared him to be a "bard of beauty".[19] Clément himself often spoke of how he had discovered that one could show the existence of God by means of beauty. He believed that Christian writers and poets had a specific *diakonia* to exercise. Just as the deacon serves as intermediary between priest and people, so the writer too should be a servant, one who demonstrates the sacramental character of a certain type of beauty that is inseparable from love and the revelation of "persons". It was thus fitting that in the same homily Metropolitan Emmanuel described Clément as "a *deacon* of the Word". In "passing on" the real treasures of Orthodoxy, this *passeur* sought to decipher the divine beauty in all places and all people and attempted to catch a glimpse of it in his many published pages—pages on which the watermark of his own profound spirituality is not hard to detect.

---

[16] See, for example, O. Clément, *Byzance et le christianisme* (Paris: Presses Universitaires de France, 1964), 60.
[17] See for example, Clément, *Le Visage intérieur*, 39
[18] *Ibid.*, 63.
[19] See *Contacts*, 228 (2009), 389.

Connected with beauty are other leitmotivs, such as the theme of *transfiguration* and in particular Clément's special gift for sensitizing us to the *cosmic dimension* of the Incarnation. But enough has been said to show that, though his writings are not systematic, we cannot deny their cohesiveness.

Olivier Clément lived and worked in the centre of Paris—the "City of Light", as the champions of the so-called Enlightenment call it. Reading this spiritual autobiography, however, we come to understand why and how this boy from the sun-baked Midi learned to sing, in the words of the title of the present book, of that *Other Sun*: Christ, the True Light.[20]

Note: The French original comes as one long text. The chapter divisions and headings are those of the translator.

---

[20] Cf. Jn 1:29.

✜ 1 ✜

Childhood and Youth

I LIKE LISTENING TO PEOPLE TALK ABOUT THEMSELVES. Talking about myself, on the other hand, is not something I enjoy. The only important thing, it seems to me, is that sudden change of heart which makes the future possible. "Go and sin no more", says Jesus to the adulterous woman after he has saved her from being stoned. Everything is new again. Death is no more. Death—that mirror in which we continually gaze at ourselves. Which is why I feel it impossible to talk about myself; for I know now that the mirror has been shattered. However, I would like to try to talk about *him*. About how he seeks us out. About how he sought *me* out, and found me.

In Dostoevsky's novel *The Adolescent*, there is a man who has lost everything—his youth, his wife, his house—and who wanders about with no fixed abode, living on nothing, sleeping under the stars in summer, purifying his heart, progressing towards the "place of the heart". And a lot of time is required, a lot of ground needs to be covered in order to reach what Lorenzatos called this "lost center".[1] One morning he wakes up in the middle of a field. It is very early; everything is

---

[1] See Zissimos Lorenzatos, *The Lost Center and Other Essays in Greek Poetry*, trans. Kay Cicellis (Princeton: Princeton University Press, 1980).

light and airy, new, original. Another sun is illumining creation, as if for a day that knows no evening. And, no doubt for the first time, he sees, he understands, he perceives and welcomes the "mystery" of everything. He woke up at sunrise; he awakes now to that Other Sun. Now he sees that the essence of things is prayer, and that man is to gather and express it. "The grass grows … Grow, grass of God."[2] At such moments a sacred feeling of awe pierces the heart. It was the feeling I had when, as a child on the deserted beach in winter, I would enjoy digging in the sand until the sky turned upside down, until right at the bottom of my hole there appeared a round pool of water that reflected another light. Yes, life is a mystery and "that it's a mystery makes it only the better; it fills the heart with awe and wonder and this awe maketh glad the heart".

This wanderer, who is called Makar—a name meaning "blessed" in the sense used in the Beatitudes: "Blessed are the meek, for they shall inherit the earth", though they inherit it already—this pilgrim Makar comes to the following conclusion: "All is in thee my Lord, and I, too, am in thee; have me in thy keeping."

It is God's apparent absence which creates a space for this "Have me". An absence that lasts until the day we understand that it is in God that our freedom lies. That it is precisely his silence which makes us free. "All is in thee; have me in thy keeping."

✥

When I was a child, they never talked to me about God. Not even when I asked—as all children

---

[2] Quotations are from part 3, ch. 1, section 3 in the translation by Constance Garnett, to which she gave the alternative title *A Raw Youth*.

do, even if nowadays they try to eradicate from their minds the very words of the question—not even when I asked why we are alive, why we die. They never spoke about him; they never spoke *to* him. Except perhaps once in their lives, at the premature death of someone close. Then those women from the tragic Cévennes, who nursed a spirit of rebelliousness that resembled some not quite cooled lava, would suddenly erupt in a long string of blasphemies during which their whole being would fall apart.[3]

They didn't speak about God, the living God. But god—the word "god"—was often what it has ceased to be today: a topic of conversation. Today people are no longer embarrassed to talk about sex, only about God. On Sundays the clan would assemble, at least those members who had settled in town. Or, rather, every other Sunday. On the intervening Sundays our family would go back to the village.[4] So one Sunday in two, my mother's sisters—who were primary-school teachers—came to dinner at our house. (Down there "dinner" is what Parisians would call "lunch".) My uncle the hauler, too. He who spent his life hobbling along the roads of Languedoc on his wooden leg, because his wagons were horse-drawn and he had to hold the lead horse by the bridle. He knew all about cooking, having learned it in the wayside inns that the haulers frequented. Often, to celebrate, he would

---

[3] The Cévennes are a range of mountains known for its large community of Protestants, or Huguenots. During the reign of Louis XIV, when much of the Huguenot population fled France, those in the Cévennes largely remained where they were, protected to some extent by the hilly terrain and energized by their fierce spirit of independence.

[4] The town was Montpellier, the village Marsillargues. It is in this village that Olivier Clément's grave is located.

bring a mute, or Muscovy, duck. The mute ones are the best, he used to say. Then there was my other uncle, who was a station employee. Many of those who had moved down from the Cévennes were hired by the state railway company.

The conversation was lively and frank. It was the women, intellectual and independent, who called the tune. With great delight, I would wait for the dessert and the inevitable discussion on the existence of God. My aunts were deists in the tradition of Jules Ferry,[5] whereas my parents—who were also primary-school teachers—had become atheists at the time of militant Combism.[6] Nobody got annoyed, nobody tried to convince anyone else. It was more like a friendly musical performance, and God stayed put inside the most profane of language. Voices were only lowered, only became excited when the talk turned to the mysteries of love, or politics, or illness—especially tuberculosis. On no account must the *petite* marry someone with tuberculosis. The Supreme Being—who must himself already have been very sick since he seemed incapable of sorting everything out and refused to

---

[5] Jules Ferry (1832–93) was a freemason and statesman who became prime minister. His name is associated not only with colonial expansion but also education. It is the Jules Ferry Laws of 1881 and 1882 that are credited with the creation of the modern republican school, in which education (from the primary stage upwards) is free and mandatory, but non-clerical. These laws also repealed most of the Falloux Laws of 1850–1, which had given an important role to the clergy,

[6] Émile Combes (1835–1921)—ex-seminarian turned atheist and fiercely anti-Catholic—was another statesman who became head of the government. His aggressive, anti-clerical campaign led to the 1905 Law of the Separation of Church and State, which, among other things, completed the secularization of education.

perform miracles everywhere like they said he did at Lourdes—well, this phantom Being vanished into thin air at some point between the smell of the coffee and the first tinkling of the washing up.

I gained nothing from these conversations, just the rumour of an absence.

Silences proved to be more important. The nursery school, where one of my aunts lived as well as worked, was one vast zone of silence on Thursday afternoons and on Sundays.[7] It was as if the screaming, gesticulating children had themselves sculpted this silence. At the end of spring I would wait for the evening clamour caused by thousands of sparrows as they descended on the plane trees and acacias that grew in the playground. Once the mild evening air had been fully infused with the darkness of night and the first star had appeared, the sparrows would all begin to chirp at once. The trees crackled, as it were, with unseen sparks. I learned later that in the early days of Christianity it was believed that at certain times of day the animals themselves began to pray.

Sometimes I got on my bicycle and pedalled off to the sea.

More important than my aunts' school was the village where my father's family lived, and where we often went to my grandparents'. Every fortnight on Sundays, as mentioned. Every holiday, too. In this village, which was situated between the vineyards and the *étangs*[8]—the vineyards constituting an obvious feature,

---

[7] Thursdays because, until as late as 1972, no afternoon lessons were given on that day, though schools were open on Saturdays.

[8] The word *étang* (normally translated as "pond") refers here to an expanse of brackish water separated from the Mediterranean by a narrow strip of sand. A string of these lagoons stretches

the *étangs* being more secret places—the locals would tell you that three "religions" existed side by side: you had the Catholics, the Protestants and the "socialists". A "socialist", in the special sense the word then had in this region, was someone who never went into a church, whether Catholic or Protestant. If his daughter were unfortunately to be planning a church wedding, and if he agreed not to quarrel, he would remain conspicuously on the threshold with the village youth, preparing in manly fashion the detonation of rifle shots that would greet the newly married couple as they emerged. So, a "socialist" never went to church, did not have his children baptized and had himself been married in the town hall. (He also remained faithful to his wife, indeed obeyed her—as is fitting in a so-called "patriarchal" society.) Nor did he bury his dead with any religious rites, though he was scrupulous in holding a wake for them. In this region there are no crosses in the cemeteries. The Protestants—who were for long in the majority and socially dominant—bitterly hated the cross. At Nîmes in the sixteenth century, at the time of the great religious conflicts, it was not unknown for dogs to be crucified.

During the Revolution, the Wars of Religion had flared up again but by my grandparents' day, the "socialists" had ousted the Protestants and gained control of the town council. The establishment of the Third Republic in 1870 had enabled people to take revenge. The Rue de l'Église had been renamed the Rue Karl Marx and a urinal had been built against the apse of the church.[9] The church itself dates from 1688.

along the southern French coast from the Rhone delta to the foothills of the Pyrenees.

[9] This detail inevitably reminds one of *Clochemerle*, the immensely popular 1934 satirical novel by Gabriel Chevallier.

The date is inscribed on the porch—evidence of a violent reconquest following the Revocation of the Edict of Nantes, for the entire population had gone over to the Reformation in the sixteenth century. No sign of Christ on this porch; just the proud symbol of the Sun King shining down on a subject planet.[10] Legends about Cathars were unheard of. (Those enamoured of Occitan language and culture—and who nowadays wear secondary-school teachers down—should be reminded of this.) These legends were invented later by anticlerical primary-school teachers, and about an area much further to the West, the other side of Béziers. Nevertheless, all the tragedies of Western Christianity had left their mark. The château had belonged to Guillaume de Nogaret, who, for the glory of the king, or the nation, had slapped the Pope across the face—a pope who had claimed to be Emperor, too. The Pope died as a result, added my grandfather, when he told me this story.[11] Anti-Reformation persecution

> This perceptive, Rabelaisian caricature of French society as it was in 1923 takes as its connecting thread the squabbles that engulf an entire village and even the higher authorities (traditionalists and free-thinkers alike) as a result of the mayor's plans to install a urinal just by the church. Whether he knew it or not, it seems that Chevallier's fiction is not entirely divorced from fact.

[10] As Olivier Clément wrote these lines—charting his progression from the Sun of the Mediterranean to the Sun of Righteousness, Christ the true King—the ironical aspect of Louis XIV's choice of nickname will not have been lost on him.

[11] Guillaume de Nogaret (1260–1313) was councillor and Keeper of the Seal to Philip IV. The Pope in question—Boniface VIII—had declared that temporal as well as spiritual power was under his jurisdiction, and that kings were subordinate to him. Nogaret had gone to Rome with a small army intent on capturing the Pope and bringing him to France, where a council would be convened with the intent of deposing him.

had left its mark everywhere in this region, where Protestantism had spread throughout the population of all the mountain villages and even overflowed down as far as the *étangs*. A French-speaking Protestantism, by the way, for although the Bible has been translated into just about every language under the sun, it has never been translated into the local language, Occitan, the *langue d'oc*.¹² French was also the language used by the local socialists at the beginning of the century. Grandfather was relaxed about his bilingualism, although when it was a question of socialism he always thought and spoke in French. Just as my ancestors from the Cévennes had sung, in French, to Marot's texts about the thirsting of the spiritual deer and about the God of hosts, not just heavenly but earthly.¹³

Grandfather would often tell me about the events of 1907, in which he had played a certain role.¹⁴ He

> The Pope was captured and imprisoned in Rome. He was freed after two days, but did indeed die only a month later. Nowadays he is best remembered for his feud with Dante who, in his *Divine Comedy*, placed him in the eighth Circle of Hell among those guilty of simony.

¹² The first translation of the Bible into Occitan was published in Toulouse as recently as 2013.

¹³ Clément Marot (1496–1544) was an important poet of Protestant sympathies whose lyrics have been popular with musicians. His output included versifications of the Psalms in French—and this at a time when the use of the vernacular was frowned upon. Nonetheless, they were extremely popular and influenced Calvin's reform of church music, a reform which allowed for nothing but the unaccompanied congregational singing of psalms.

¹⁴ After the disastrous effects of phylloxera and the slow process of restocking the vineyards, there followed an over-production of inexpensive wine. The price plummeted. Then cheap wine began to be imported, from Algeria in particular. To top it all, fraudulent wines were allowed to be marketed, affecting the livelihood of coopers, glassmakers and traders as well

definitely saw it as being a social and economic crisis, but didn't associate it with any specifically Occitan demands. In fact, in his opinion such demands were more the concern of the extreme right-wing. (I include this little digression so as to ruffle the feathers of present-day promoters of Occitan language and culture, who do make essential points all the same.)

So, evidence of how the Reformation had been suppressed was everywhere. When digging among the vines, you would sometimes find human bones—the remains of Protestants who, prior to the Edict of Toleration of 1787, were not allowed to be buried in the cemeteries. Not far from grandfather's village, near the *étangs*, was an enormous tower. I liked to climb right to the top, from where you had a view of the entire region, from the sea to the mountains with, to the north-west, Mont Aigoual, "the watery one",[15] and to the north-east, "the windy one", the Mont Ventoux. I had been told that in the eighteenth century Protestant women—often those from the Cévennes, like my mother—would be shut up in this tower. One of them, who had been incarcerated when aged eighteen and only let out again at the age of sixty, had engraved the word *résister* on a coping stone. I would trace over each

as growers. Throughout 1907 regular demonstrations were held, growing in size. Things came to a head in June of that year when between six hundred and eight hundred thousand people of all political persuasions gathered in Montpellier. Six hundred mayors supported the people by resigning simultaneously. Churches and cathedrals opened their doors to accommodate protesters who had travelled from afar. It was only after seven demonstrators had been shot by the military that the government agreed to take action.

[15] Situated in a major water catchment area of the Massif Central. It is the heavy rainfall that has given the mountain its name, originally *Aqualis*.

letter with my finger. Oddly enough, instead of the first *s* she had put a *g*. (I discovered later that in her local dialect this verb is pronounced *régister*.[16]) One word, they told me, one word would have been enough for her to have been released. But she never uttered it.

"Why?"

"A matter of conscience."

There was much talk of conscience in the "secular" education I received.[17] There was, for example, the image of a little girl in an immaculate smock that a single lie would be enough to make dirty.[18] And even if some poor devil, panting and gasping, should take refuge in your house and even if the assassins hunting him down should knock at your door and question you, would it be permissible to lie to them? I didn't know then that this example can be found in Kant. But I did know that, if you did lie, the immaculate smock would be sullied—sullied for ever. For, in fact, who was there who could forgive? Yet in the *régister* of the tower, I sensed the existence of another sort of conscience, not just moral but personal. Uncompromising. They were quick to reassure me, skipping over—as does your typical history book—the thousands of days, the thousands of nights she had spent in that tower,

---

[16] The *g* is soft, being pronounced like the *s* in *measure*.

[17] Clément's ironic stress on the adjective "secular" stems from the fact that at the period in question French state education was aggressively anti-religious, as already indicated—the village schoolmaster being the classic enemy of the village priest. The novels and films of Marcel Pagnol—*Manon des sources*, for example—contain popular presentations of this theme.

[18] Until the late 1960s, young French school children wore back-buttoning smocks. This was mainly in order to protect their clothing, though they were expected to keep the smocks clean as well.

in that prison, consumed by fevers, frozen stiff by the mistral. They skipped smartly to the triumphant conclusion: the old woman had proved stronger than the king, stronger than the Pope. As for the king, he had had his head chopped off. The Pope ... Here the uncle who worked for the railway company would snigger, "*Le Pape, le Pape?* Why not call him *la Mame?*"[19] We were very respectful in our family. Our speech was blunt, but dignified and imbued with a sense of decency — except, precisely, in matters of religion.

So, then, on the paternal side of the family — the only one I had any experience of, never having known my mother's parents — although some ancestors had been Catholic and others Protestant, we were by now up to the third generation of "socialists". It was my grandfather who had made the conscious decision to become "converted". His was a strong personality. He was a truly righteous man, almost in the biblical sense of the word. Brought up in a Catholic milieu — albeit a Catholicism that was effete and that consisted above all in unintelligible observances — he had made a painful but deliberate break, when only twelve years old. A break with what he described as a world characterized by hypocrisy, by an ill-defined domination of souls, and by an absence of virility but an obsession with sexual matters. The questions put to him in the confessional would turn his stomach. Even when well advanced in age, he would still have dreams in which he was being chased by figures in cassocks.

---

[19] *Mame* is a shortened form of *Madame* in popular language. But since *Pape* sounds like *papi, papy, papé, papet* — all being familiar terms for *grandpa, grandpapa* — the uncle might also have had in mind the corresponding terms for *granny, grandma*; namely, *mamie, mamy*.

He had married a Protestant girl and, for a while, had taken an interest in his wife's religion. However, her pastor had refused to give the slightest help to a group of agricultural labourers who were engaged in a just strike, one that was causing real hunger. So at that point grandfather persuaded his wife to follow him into becoming a "socialist". At least, as far as matters of conscience were concerned. For she had considerable reservations, and continued to be at the service of society in her own way, thinking first and foremost of her concrete "neighbour" rather than some distant, abstract humanity. And—secret of secrets!—as her husband went about his activism and campaigning, she looked on rather as an indulgent mother watches her child at play.

It was not out of class hatred that grandfather had become a socialist, but as a result of his high moral standards. He had originally been an agricultural labourer, descended from ordinary working-class folk. The girl he married worked in a hat shop, but counted among her ancestors free men who had been *gardians*, Camargue "cowboys". Thanks to the friendly owner of a *mas*, as Provençal farmhouses are called, grandfather had obtained, for almost nothing, some land near the *étangs* that could be brought into cultivation. Like many others at the time, he had become a small landowner. Patiently he had enlarged his plot of land. The Republic had made it easier for these wine-growers to become independent and had also given them schools, which enabled their children to improve their position in society. The village was a remarkably cohesive place. Grandfather was on good terms with the descendants of the former *seigneur*. Small landowner, socialist militant that he was, he felt that he too was a *seigneur*. He harboured no feelings of resentment against anyone, but was socialist in the sense of wishing to further and to spread civilization, to achieve more equality by means of co-operation, by a stronger communal way of life, and by the dispersal and spread of property. After the crisis of 1907, he had been one of the founders of the village winegrowers' co-operative, which set the growers free from the blackmailing tactics being used by the speculators. He had also managed to obtain from the municipality grants for those boys and girls who wished to continue their studies, though he had waited until his own son had finished studying before embarking on this particular campaign. He felt close to the workers, wanting them to improve their social position in the same way that he himself had, by acquiring more responsibility—a creative responsibility. He had made a considerable contribution to the funds being collected when Jean Jaurès had set up a famous self-governing workers' glassworks in Albi.[20]

Of course, grandfather was in no sense a revolutionary; he was a socialist who was firmly anchored within an existing civilization. People of his generation were *supported*. Nowadays we seem to feel we must reinvent everything, but they had their land, their language and a sort of natural goodwill and companionship. A social physiology complete with rites of communion. For instance, for the bullfights the entire village would gather on the *plan*, a level area, where rows of seats were placed. These were in fact long platforms set between tall, slender wheels. During the recent harvest season they had been used for transporting the grapes.

[20] Jean Jaurès (1859–1914) was the local deputy in the National Assembly and one of the most energetic defenders of Dreyfus. An anti-militarist, he was assassinated at the outbreak of the First World War.

Square-shaped vats were set up on these tumbrel-like contraptions, and into them the grapes were tipped. The children would run behind and jump onto the back end and drink the sticky must that brimmed over the edge of the vats.

For the bullfights, only the platforms were used. People would sit on the edges, though chairs were placed on them for the elderly. The bulls were never killed. The risk was all on the side of the humans. Young men would try to snatch a piece of the red cloth that had been tied to the beast's horns. It was Cretan in character rather than Spanish, except that the ladies stayed in their places, opening their arms to the *raseteurs*[21] — the word for the protagonists charged down by the bulls and who had had to jump right into the middle of the crowd of spectators. (In more recent times, a barrier is erected, like in Spain.) No blood, then, but a whirling mass of young men dressed in white, moving now slowly, now faster around a slim, dark-skinned beast with horns in the shape of a lyre. None of the ponderous "sacredness" of the Spanish *corrida*. Just good fun and the pleasure of all being together. The best bulls turn up time and again. They become famous, make a name for themselves. In actual fact, they are rarely genuine bulls. Mostly half-wild bullocks, old timers who have been spared the abattoir thanks to their cantankerous character. Yet there — in this contrast between sun and beast as the night closed in as an antidote to the sun — you had the essential character of the land and its secret, with man as intermediary between earth and sky.

---

[21] From a Provençal verb meaning to go as close as possible to something.

Other gatherings were occasioned by the local language. The finest took place in the setting of a rugged valley of *garrigue* scrubland near a river over which there still stood two arches of a Roman bridge. We sat on the rocky ground among bright loose stones, between clumps of wild thyme and shrub-like oaks which, set against the sun, looked almost black. Poets came to sing and recite. And there too, in this incandescent landscape, everything was done within limits, was clearly defined, safe, human. A refined lyricism, with a touch of banter. *Vin rosé* was passed round but no-one ever got drunk. What was the point, when simply to be alive was intoxication enough? And at the climax, of course, the *coupo santo*.[22] Everyone was there—right-wing, left-wing, Protestant, Catholic, "socialists", all united by the language just as they had been by the bulls. And as they also were when, in spring, whole groups would go out to gather wild narcissi in the meadows that bordered the last vineyards before you came to the marshland and then the *étang*.

In these rites of communication, there would crop up vocabulary normally associated with religion. There was, of course, the symbol of the *coupo*, the cup overflowing with the fervour of the strong. Or, more

---

[22] *Coupo santo* (Holy Cup): these are the first words of the refrain of the traditional anthem of Provence and the Languedoc, and also the name by which it has become known. The lyrics are by Mistral, the poet who was largely responsible for reviving the local language in the mid-nineteenth century. The reference is to an elaborate silver cup offered by Catalan poets and writers to their Provençal counterparts in 1867 to thank them for hiding a poet from Barcelona, who had sought political asylum. One is supposed to stand for the last verse. The song has since taken on a far wider significance, glorifying Provençal culture and history in general. It is even sung before sporting fixtures.

succinctly still, the description used of anyone passionate about *la bouvine*—that is, everything connected with the culture and traditions of the Camargue, especially its bulls and horses. "He has the faith!" they would say.

Such rites afforded protection, certainly. They also introduced you to silence. These men who were straight-talking and never short of words, these tellers of tales—like my grandfather, who would often tell me stories he had made up—were also solitary beings, taciturn, passionate about the secret spots around the *étangs* on land that had been badly desalinated and where bulls and horses roamed free. They loved to go for long rambles in the *garrigue* on the pretext, according to the season, of gathering wild asparagus, azeroles or pine cones swollen with *pignons*. You had to put these cones in the kitchen stove for a while before being able to work the pine kernels loose.

When evening drew in—except in summer when we would sit out in the street, chatting with the neighbours—we didn't light the paraffin lamp or switch on the electric light straight away. The entire household would sit in the same room in front of a fire of vine stocks. As night thickened, everyone remained silent, rough hands placed on knees. Nothing visible but the fire ... It was in this way that I had my first experience of mystery: silence, night, flames, that solemn surrender. Then suddenly, when the darkness had become oppressive, light! Like a resurrection! And then the hubbub of life, as they began to bustle about preparing the evening meal, which would be followed by a friendly evening gathering.

They were supported, these villagers, protected. They might confront one another—about socialism, say, or the existence of God—but that did not call into question something more fundamental: an underlying friendship between human beings, between things too. A modesty devoid of prudery. Fidelity in the family, the clan and the village. A sort of boundary that protected you from what was inhuman. It was impossible for just any old thing to happen at any old time. Yet all of that has been lost, because no-one took care of it. All those basic things, as basic as the air we breathe. None of the villagers would have known how to put this into words, still less how to justify it. It was simply the surrounding culture—a genuine one, in which everyone participated, but one which was only able to survive by the momentum of history. Without them realizing, it was eating away at its own spiritual capital. I sensed this quite quickly when I became a nihilist, like most young people—much sooner than many, though, thanks to my uprooting and my inner impatience. Today we are all nihilists. Even in the villages, where people take tranquilizers now just like everywhere else. More than in the towns, in fact. This is why political quarrels assume such importance, though in reality they have hardly any at all. It is the fundamental things that we must rediscover.

I am certain now that all those folk (whether pro-clerical, anti-clerical, Catholic, Protestant or "socialist") lived out their lives against a Christian background—an ancient, savoury dish of the things of the earth cooked over the fire of the Gospel. But the link with the roots had been broken, and attempts to return to the sources were becoming ever more indirect. One of them, unquestionably the last, had been the "socialism" of my grandfather and my father. But, perhaps through the fault of the Christians, this renewal had turned into a diversion. French socialism had emphasized the communal, social dimension of the Gospel that the Christians of the nineteenth century—pietistic and frightened—had somewhat forgotten. Which is why, moreover, the socialists had ended up becoming atheists. Nevertheless, in everyday life they remained influenced by that social evangelism of 1848 that the young Dostoevsky loved, because it did not reject Jesus and because, as he said, "it is not a system". The fundamental instincts of the first French socialists such as Pierre Leroux were for justice, of course, but above all for communion. "My life is yours", the novelist Georges Sand (who was influenced by him) used to say. Moreover, Leroux chose as epigraph for his main book—*De l'humanité* (1840)—St Paul's passage about the single body in which we are all "members of one another". He had this extraordinary saying, that only the mystical theology of the Eastern Church has enabled me to understand: "All human beings are like the Trinity." He was opposed to left-wing Hegelians, too. If they were to gain the upper hand, he used to say, "everyone would become a state functionary with the Inquisition at his door". To describe his movement, he proposed the term "communionism".[23]

This was still the basic attitude of Jean Jaurès, though it had become almost embarrassing for him, almost secret. He left behind some affectionate jottings about Christ and made time regularly to read not just Homer and Dante, but the Bible. He stressed the primordial importance of the spiritual life, as when he wrote of "bringing about justice in the social sphere in order to prepare for the easier access of souls to the mystical

---

[23] In the wake of the revolutionary decades of the 1790s and the Napoleonic era, the philosopher and political economist Pierre Leroux attempted to revive spirituality and social communion—though without basing things on the pillars of the old regime. His main work (*De l'humanité*) stresses the interdependence of all human beings.

sphere".[24] Much was at stake at the beginning of the twentieth century; the progress of the socialist movement, at least in France, was still uncertain. Sorel's "ethic of the producers" revealed a touching nostalgia for the early Church, for a similar capacity genuinely to change lives—between people as well as within each person—and, in a social fabric that had become necrotic, to multiply places of communion, of genuine freedom and of beauty.[25] Only, rather than fostering a creative Christianity, a Christianity of divine-humanity, the movement had come up against a Marxism of the most dogmatic sort.

There was Péguy, of course: "To all appearances, our socialism [...] was a sort of Christianity".[26] In the

[24] See *La Question sociale, l'injustice du capitalisme et la révolution religieuse* (1891).

[25] Georges Sorel (1847–1922) was a philosopher and sociologist known both for his theory of revolutionary syndicalism and his writings on the importance of the moral aspects of social movements. His reconstruction of socialist ethics established him as a remarkable critic of Marxist thought. The phrase quoted by Clément—"the ethic of the producers"—is from the 1908 book *Réflections sur la violence*. It refers to Sorel's hope and belief that strikes would bring capitalism to an end, but would replace it not by state socialism but by a society of producers.

[26] Charles Péguy (1873–1914) was a Catholic poet, philosopher, essayist and editor who combined Christianity with socialism and patriotism. Péguy's words are quoted by Daniel Halévy, a friend and editorial collaborator, in his *Charles Péguy et les Cahiers de la Quinzaine* (Paris: Payot, 1918), 21. The quotation is taken from a passage in which Halévy records Péguy's own account of his time. When at the Collège Sainte-Barbe in Paris, he was influenced by the dynamic school chaplain (who was himself influenced by the 1891 encyclical *Rerum novarum*). Péguy and a group of friends would travel to the poor suburbs to perform acts of charity. His Catholicism was, as he put it, a "social Catholicism". Similarly—which is the point of the above quotation—his "socialism" took no account of doctrine or the Party. Indeed, he very soon dissociated himself entirely

Orthodox world there was Berdyaev, Bulgakov and certain intuitions of Makrakis.[27] But these were isolated prophets, at a time when nihilism (which had also had its solitary heralds in the nineteenth century) was on the point of making history with the First World War and what would later become known as the Gulag. These prophets of a creative Christianity were overpowered. Killed. Cast onto other soil like so many torn off seed heads. Defeated? I think not. It is certain that they will prevail in the end, since it is not possible to build on nothingness. And since Christ is risen.

✣

Grandfather died like one of the just—stoically, clear-headed, refusing to be deceived about his condition. He died at home, among his own. I have the impression that he would have liked to have given his blessing, but didn't know how. Infinitely tactful, he was afraid of upsetting the children by the sight of his mortal remains. He was wrong: children like the silence and peace of the dead. Without any boastfulness, without any confidence either, he claimed he was ready to meet God, if God existed. But it seems he meant the god of morality. The life of this lean, grey-eyed southerner had been as clean as a blade, as clean as a ploughshare. (I had noticed that ploughshares were never dirtied by the clay.) To the end, he had borne witness to what he believed in, though without fanaticism. After the

---

from socialist ideology, disapproving of its anticlericalism and its materialism.

[27] Apostolos Makrakis (1831–1905), lay theologian, preacher, ethicist and philosopher, was a leader of the "awakening movement" in the period following the Greek War of Independence. Though prolific and charismatic, he was also controversial.

war and the Russian Revolution, he had refused to go over to communism, which reminded him too much, he said, of Catholicism—meaning the Inquisition. He was too well supported by a civilization to be in need of this replacement form of absolutism. What's more, he had been shocked by the ethical relativism of the local communists in the village. For him, as for my father, nothing could justify lies or perjury.

Grandfather left behind two children: my father, who became a schoolmaster and moved to the town; and my aunt, the one who still lived in the village. She was a seamstress and preoccupied with her garden. With them came the time of silence.

My father was a just man, like grandfather. But he had lost touch with the land, the language, the whole ebb and flow of life in the village, an entire culture. One that was anyway falling apart under the blows of wars, "total" politics, and an ultimately pointless technology. He was a socialist, but only by heredity. Was he still a socialist by the time he reached fifty? As a young man he had campaigned alongside anarcho-syndicalists, but had been disillusioned. He had picked up the smell of the "strong beast" that Plato spoke of in connection with mass action. Even in a righteous city there are some who will always be bruised by collective life, for they carry within themselves a silence, a nostalgia, an empty space that society cannot fill. My father was one of these. He had inherited the brown eyes and extreme gentleness of his mother who, at the end of her life, cradled the emptiness within her while humming softly all the while.

It was during the war, when faced with death, that my father discovered naked, undisguised friendship. When the war was over, so were the friendships. Everyone went home. And anyway that kind of friendship had about it a taste of horror. What had still kept him going was his profession and his family. But it was no longer a village family, one whose life was the neighbourhood. It too was immersed in a community that was all-embracing, but differently so. It was a self-contained town family. In a world built by women for children, father got bogged down in family worries. He got bogged down, he suffocated, he remained silent. A parishioner without a parish, a contemplative to whom no-one had ever spoken about the living God.

As a child, he had loved to read the Book of Revelation. (When one has Protestant ancestors—and for this they deserve thanks—the house is always full of bibles.) "How stupid I was!" he would say. "How stupid! But it was so beautiful, that heavenly Jerusalem!" He hardly ever spoke about his most important experiences, his experiences of this heavenly Jerusalem which never ceases to descend into the heart of things. He never talked about them. Almost never. Just once, when we were harvesting the grapes together. I was an adolescent at the time. I would cut bunches of them and then, with each cartful, go to the wine cellar to gauge the percent proof of the must. In the early morning, like some crazy lover, you plunge your hands into the enormous piles dripping with dew, down as far as the bunches that have become heavy and sticky. Or else you listen to the must as it ferments, intoxicated with the aroma like a honeybee. In the wine cellar all is dark and, almost imperceptibly, the secret song of metamorphosis rises from the depths of the liquid as it quivers into life: the world as sacrament. Then, just as deep, you experience a feeling of sheer fatigue along with the knowledge and calming of the body that it brings. And each evening, after bathing in the river and putting on light clothing, you feel emerging from within you a bud of real life.

At such moments one is able to listen, and to speak. And so it was that my father began to tell me a little about himself. It happened during the war, at the time of Verdun. He had just spent fifteen days in the trenches, in shell holes, in that desert landscape where neither the terrain nor the night afforded protection any more, violated as they were by the heavy gunfire and the shaking caused by the explosions. You could no longer sleep, or talk. Then the survivors had been removed and given a rest period. After a long sleep, father got out of bed. It was one morning in spring. He set off alone into the Lorraine forest. Suddenly he found himself in a clearing. Clusters of flowers ... An awesome silence ... Then all at once the sound of bells from an invisible steeple. The man burst into tears. He didn't go any further. The solitude, the clearing dotted with flowers, the silence, the song of the bells, the tears ... He was overcome by an all-pervading feeling of adoration. He wasn't able to put it into words. Jerusalem, Jerusalem in the forest of Lorraine, with bells proclaiming a resurrection. I have tried to find the words myself. And now, along with him who died while still relatively young and whom I wounded when I broke up the enclosed world that supported him and in which he suffocated, with him I dare to pronounce the words: death, hell, resurrection. Death and a love stronger than death. Not morality, nor the pseudo-transcendence of emasculation, but a life stronger than death. Resurrection!

Once. He talked to me in this way just that once. Otherwise he kept silent. He read books, though. Strange books that he talked to no-one about, but that I discovered in his very interesting library. *The Brothers*

Karamazov by Dostoevsky, *Father Sergius* by Tolstoy, *La Vie de saint Serge* by Boris Zaitsev.[28] (Zaitsev was the grandfather of Michel Sollogoub, who was to become my friend. How strangely our destinies are woven together! And yet there is no such thing as destiny. It is God who does the weaving, as long as we let him.[29])

Father remained silent. He lived in a family, but he remained silent. His sister lived alone in the village, and she too kept silent. But the things around her, especially her plants, were full of life. She was an atheist, of course, like her father. But in the drawer where she kept the things she cherished, I found a copy of St John's Gospel. St John's Gospel ... *La Vie de Saint Serge* ... It was their secret, just as Jaurès's faith had become his secret. All in all, I was witness to this major occurrence: the disappearance of all language to do with God and, simultaneously, the end of a culture.

When I think of that twilight ritual, that protracted silence around the fireside, it seems that I was living in another world, one just as remote as those studied by ethnologists. As a matter of fact, it is in museums now that I sometimes come across familiar objects from my village childhood. Or else—which is worse and which, as I see it, is the very expression of nihilism—I come across them transformed into lamp-stands or other knick-knacks. Cartwheels were designed to revolve, you idiots, not support flower pots!

Diverse as it was, this culture—and I have mentioned only one of its forms—did not break down

---

[28] Written in 1925, this biography appeared in a French translation in 1928 in *Le Roseau d'or*, a journal edited by Jacques Maritain.
[29] Michel Sollogoub, Professor Emeritus of Economy of the University of Paris I–Panthéon Sorbonne, has also been a member of the editorial board of the review *Contacts*.

at the same time everywhere. For many sections of French society, especially the Christians, it is still a contemporary event. It is probably the difficult but ultimately beneficial testing of one's freedom. People become aware of having reached the end of the road and turn to replacement "religions", political or other. Yet signs of a renewed Christianity are also starting to appear.

The prophetic power of the great Russians such as Dostoevsky derives from the fact that they experienced all this a good century before we did. Probably because in Russia there was no humanist tradition. Whatever the case, a century before us they went to the limits of atheism. We, for our part, managed for a long time to turn "atheism" into a topic of conversation, a literary theme—a wonderful *morbo literario*, the morbid literary curiosity of civilized people! We remained protected, too, by a certain peasant wisdom, by our old-fashioned style of life, and our traditional games. The great Russians, however, encountering head on the full force of the atheism of our Western theories, had already tasted of hell, death—and resurrection.

Father's paradisal clearing, the paschal peal of bells … Remember Dostoevsky in penal exile after the hell of an imminent march to the gallows. Remember the house of the dead.[30] Suddenly he too hears the bells of Pascha and the certainty of the living God takes hold of him, a God crucified and yet the conqueror of death: "He exists! He exists!" Since then, the whole of Russia has experienced a descent into hell. Nevertheless, witnesses of resurrection do come from over there. The paradoxical advantage of our era is that history

---

[30] Dostoevsky's four-year exile of hard labour in Siberia would lead to the composition of *The House of the Dead* in 1854.

itself is pushing us into making the ultimate choice. It's either the muzzle of the gun or the foot of the cross, as the fin-de-siècle Decadents used to say. Since then, the muzzle of the gun has assumed strange proportions. We are all in its sights.

So, *La Vie de Saint Serge* and St John's Gospel were really their secret. God was becoming the great secret of our times. No-one had ever talked to me about him and, I should add, even less about Christ. When, aged probably seven or eight, I had asked my father the key questions—"Why do we live? Why do we die?"—he had replied: "After we die, there's nothing. But all the same, one should try to be good, to be fair and honest".

"What about other people? How do they behave?"

"Well, you know, people follow their own interests. But, still, one should ..."

When responding to these sorts of questions, what sprang spontaneously to my father's lips was the ideology of the *écoles normales* of the beginning of the century, tinged with a touch of stale socialism. As for the fundamental things—the things that he searched for in *La Vie de Saint Serge*—he didn't have the language. Just one word was all he had to formulate and set the seal on his philosophy: nothingness.

Once with my big sister—she is ten years older than me—I was passing under a fine eighteenth-century bridge that connects the old town to the hill, where a promenade had been landscaped in such a way that it takes you up by stages into ever more light.

"This bridge," I asked, "is it old?"

"Oh, yes! It was built in the time of Louis XV. Lots of people have seen it before us, lots more will see it after us."

"What will happen to us then?"

"Well, you see, we'll be dead."

"What *is* death?"
"Nothingness."
For a second or so I could no longer breathe. But, as I had already learned, if you breathe deeply whilst pulling on the skin of your stomach, you can lessen a little the feeling of anxiety.

Good people, learned people, you who spend your entire university careers without committing suicide—though some of your students do!—you who are supposedly engaged in studying the rich depths of language, you consider it only in itself. For, as you teach, it refers only to itself, doesn't it? All is discontinuity, difference, *différance*, deferral, indifference. Good people, learned people, imagine! I never needed to ask anybody the meaning, the non-meaning, the absence of meaning of the word "nothingness".[31]

So when we die, there is nothing. All those I love, all those whom I know a little, are all going to die. I counted and recounted the number of years they still had left to live—at best, at worst, at best. They're all going to die. They won't all be able to get to know each other, they won't have time: they're going to die. All those from before are dead, all those coming after will die. We lived near a railway station at the time. There were trains full of faces that I would never be able to see. Walls haunted me. Who lives on the other side? And even if I knew the answer for this particular wall, at the bottom of the courtyard there would be more walls, always more. On one occasion the pupils from my school were taken to the municipal theatre to see a folklore troupe from Central Europe. I was attracted

---

[31] In this paragraph Clément is satirizing the theories of such thinkers as Michel Foucault and Jacques Derrida, whose writings had recently become fashionable in France.

to one of the dancers that I had caught a glimpse of, but now she was gone for ever. In the schoolyard I kept sculpting things for her out of friable stones, and would bury them in a ritual of despair. My beloved stars suddenly began to fill me with terror, for I was told that their light had gone out perhaps thousands of years ago and that we were actually looking at mere phantoms. During the night, I would be awakened by a feeling of anxiety. Something, someone was sitting on my chest in the dark, suffocating me. I called it "nothingness"; now, I know its real name. I could no longer cope with the precarious pulsing of my blood that echoed in my pillow. I would run to the window, and there were the dead stars, the absurd infinity, space going on and on, no top, no bottom, void upon void, on every side a chasm into which you would fall down and down without ever stopping, uttering a silent cry.

"But beyond the stars," I had asked, "what is there?"
"More darkness, more stars."
"But further still?"
"More, still more, without end, without end ..."

And so in my own way I experienced that which, since the seventeenth century, has wreaked havoc in the West, and through it little by little the entire world: the black emptiness of the sky. And the announcement placed in Christ's mouth by Jean Paul and Vigny: heaven is empty, there is nothing there but death.[32] Later on I was to read the cry of Nietzsche's Madman:

---

[32] In *Siebenkäs*, the most famous novel of the German writer Johann Paul Friedrich Richter (known as Jean Paul), published 1796–7, there is a section entitled "The dead Christ proclaims that there is no God". In Alfred de Vigny's poem *Le Mont des Oliviers* (1843), the poet's own pessimistic, fatalistic philosophy causes him to radically deform Christ's prayer in Gethsemane. When he raises his eyes and calls on his Father, "the heavens

What were we doing when we unchained this earth from its sun? Whither is it moving now? Whither are we moving? Away from all suns? Are we not plunging continually? Backward, sideward, forward, in all directions? Is there still any up or down? Are we not straying as through an infinite nothing? Do we not feel the breath of empty space? Has it not become colder? Is not night continually closing in on us?[33]

The experience of evil—that daily coinage of death—assailed me little by little. I saw suffering and physical degeneration that led me to no deeper understanding of existence. The death of people still young, as well. Historical evil, too. Unemployment, economic strangulation, the rise of totalitarianism and war. All of it took on for me the grey colour of nothingness, grey like those areas of urban waste ground where I had started to wander.

Nothing to be done about it, either. I had never entered a church; the idea would never have crossed my mind. They could have closed down all the churches and I wouldn't have noticed. The first time I visited Paris, I was about ten years old. My parents visited lots of churches. Out of a sense of "cultural" duty, I suppose, though my father was perhaps seeking something else in these empty buildings. I tagged along, bored. The only thing that fascinated me were the columns in Notre Dame, those slender bundles that rise up and up, seeming to disappear into the

    remain dark and God does not answer". In the published version (of 1862) Vigny added a section actually entitled "Silence", ended with a reference to the "silence éternel de la Divinité".

[33] Nietzsche, *The Gay Science*, trans. Walter Kaufmann (New York: Random House, 1974). See Book III, §125.

shadows. The god of Gothic architecture has already been banished to heaven. And heaven is empty, I knew that. The pillars of Notre Dame, for me, were like an architectural fireworks display let off into the void.

A much older memory finds me in a square surfaced with black asphalt and where there was a huge crucifix tinged with verdigris. On the crucifix was a dead man. Above his head was an inscription: INRI. I thought it was the man's name, as I did have a cousin called Henri. At the foot of the crucifix was coiled a serpent, holding an apple in its mouth. I liked this display of a spiral around an axis, and also the fine tracery of the veins of the leaves that were still attached to the stalk. But what I noticed above all was that the man was dead.

Christians—I must specify: Western Christians— why have you depicted Jesus everywhere as a corpse, as a dead body devoid of hope? He who is the conqueror of death! Jesus' body was at no time a mere corpse; the Spirit never ceased to permeate it. One summer three years ago, we spent a few weeks in a Pyrenean valley, wonderful in its soft greens and greys. It is still—or, at least, for a very long time used to be—a Christian area. Everywhere there were crucifixes of grey stone. And a dead Jesus. My little son, who was about three years old at the time, went from corpse to corpse. I could no longer say to him "Christ is risen!" These crucifixes gave the lie to my words. Death was swallowing up life. At least, that's the way it looked to him. And for a long time that was the way I saw it too.

✣

I am walking along an avenue of almond trees with a friend. He is talking to me about history, the ascent of life, progress. He can't decide which is more important, happiness or prosperity.

"Personally," I say to him, "I don't give a d—."

"About what?"

"All of it! There are just people. Even if we could each live for a thousand years—a million—what would be the point, if everything must eventually be swallowed up by nothingness? What's the point of anything? Or are we supposed to forget? So everything exists just to be forgotten? But we don't forget. It isn't true. We can't forget.

And yet God was there—"He who shall come again". In my very anxiety, first of all. And also in my stubborn, almost ill-mannered, refusal to forget, to accept that this was really the way things were. Whoever accepts as self-evident that the world has been hijacked by death ceases to be human.

God came in my anxiety, then, but also in my sense of wonder. I loved the earth with a love that was serious and passionate, indulging at times in unsophisticated raptures. I would spread myself out on her and—all the lighter for being so heavy—she would carry me off as if on a pair of wings, into the wind, into the sky.

There before me was a boundless, limpid vista. The world as on the dawn of creation, it seemed, barely emerged from the sea and still half-covered in *étangs*, beaches, dunes and reeds. A vibrant vastness with winds that were ever changing under the full blessing of the open sky. Its quivering blueness is a shade deeper when seen through the pine trees. In spring the vines, with their young golden leaves, are like flaming torches and the soil the colour of ochre. The light is slowly distilled amid the splendour of the almond blossom and the vivid ivory-white of the wild narcissi. The mountains seem to be sculpted straight from the naked light. Everywhere there is a secret at the heart of the visible, a mystery amid the excess of luminosity.

On certain days at the end of winter the sea breezes and those coming from inland balance each other out. All is still. The first almond trees have flowered, with their perfect, fragile beauty set amid the peaceful, endless expanse of azure-blue sky. The blossom emerges as if straight from the wood. Flowers without leaves, born of hardness. Dry, dead, black skeletons flowering at the first breeze, like the dry bones in Ezekiel's prophecy. The Hebrew word for an almond tree comes from a root meaning to "watch" or "waken". Watcher, awakener.[34] Wakened from winter, awakening us to the beauty of all that is.

At such moments you hardly dare make a step. All sudden gestures must be avoided, for the world has become crystal-like. The slightest careless gesture might profane it, might perhaps shatter it.

However, I preferred the afternoons when the mistral roared. *Lou magistrau*: the master! Then, the wind is everywhere, coming from all directions at once, consuming all before it, even the rock, even your bones, your very being. It consumes man to his very core. It does not admit of the slightest weakness nor any ambivalence, however furtive. All is aflame, but with flames that are cold, pure and baptismal, like water.

This landscape is dry and pure with nothing glaucous or misty about it. "Earth of light, Sky of Earth", as Lorca said.[35] In the *garrigue* even what is vegetal seems mineral. How I hated the over-green Île-de-

---

[34] In the original there is here a play on words: *veilleur/éveilleur*. The same word play is found in Jeremiah 1:11–12.
[35] The refrain from the poem "El paso de la siguiriya" ("Dancing the siguiriya").

France where absolutely everything seems vegetal, and damp, even the rock, even the sky, which is like a dense, overbearing, fleshy thing. In the Mediterranean region, on the other hand, as soon as you reach the deserted plateaus the landscape seems composed of crystallized fire. Even flesh seems celestial.

In short, I was a Mediterranean pagan. To breathe, to eat, to walk—everything was experienced with passion. Was I a polytheist? It was rather a case of simply being intensely aware that things *are*. The wind gets up, the plane tree begins to sing. I know that the plane tree *is*. The day I first knew that I knew I set off walking and walking, and when evening came I was still pacing up and down in the living room, where a wood fire was burning like in the old days during the evening ritual. The consciousness of being conscious filled me with delight. It was a different form of knowledge, a kind of joy, ecstasy perhaps, but hard, crystalline, compressed like the tough texture of wood or like this stone that I hold in my hand. Yes, the secret within the visible. And I would say to myself—it was the beginning of my adolescence—"To be! To be! The kingdom of Being!" In fact, *The Kingdom of Being* was the title I had given to a collection of poems I had written and about which I have forgotten everything except that, in three cycles, it celebrated the *étangs* and the beaches, the vineyards and the *garrigue*.

Anxiety and a sense of wonder went hand in hand, then, in the same way that in the *garrigue* the leaves are hard and glossy on one side and yet light and soft on the other. And so, in a rudimentary way, I progressed from what the old spiritual masters call the "remembrance of death" to the wonder of existence. Perhaps it was an implicit foreshadowing of what I later became aware of as death-and-resurrection. But if there were to be no significant breakthrough, would not death have the last word?

Once, however, in a moment of desperate kindness—someone I was very fond of was grief-stricken and I could do nothing to help—so, once, spontaneously, fully aware of what I was doing, I said a prayer. I prayed to "God". I knew that word, thanks to the Sunday discussions. And a kind of celebration, a kind of gratitude, welled up amid the wonder.

At school, when I was about seven years old, we had been asked what the cold days and rain of November made us think about. It was a written task. I had replied: "I think about all the dead people. It makes me pray." A minor scandal ensued. The dead are nice and warm in the ground, the teacher explained. They have no need of anything. We should think, rather, of the poor, of those who have no means of keeping themselves warm. It was true. I was convinced by his words. And yet, the dead are so near to us when everything closes in during the cold season. If only we knew the way.

Nobody seemed to know that Someone had said, "I am the Way".

Later, when reading *The Way of a Pilgrim*, I came across the following lines with a sense of recognition:

> It is said in the New Testament that human beings and the whole of creation [...] naturally sigh, yearn and desire to enter into the freedom of the children of God. This sighing of creation, this innate yearning of souls is interior prayer... It is in everyone and everything![36]

✣

---

[36] See *The Pilgrim's Tale*, trans. T. Allan Smith (New York: Paulist Press, 1999), 88.

This God who came in my wonderment and my anxiety, and to whom I had prayed for an instant in my childhood—well, I forgot all about him. Or, rather, I tried to struggle against him. Of course, it is quite normal for adolescence to be a time of rejection, but rarely rejection of rejection. In my case, I rejected secular morality which is itself a rejection—a rejection of religion—and yet secular morality was the only more or less positive legacy that I had received. It is a rigid, narrow, "pure" morality. But once the culture that supported it had died, it seemed empty and without any personal or ontological basis. From then on I wished to be faithful—faithful to the point of infidelity—to one requirement only: *for me, duty is that which I need in order to exist.* I didn't know then that man is a bundle of contradictions and that it is only divine revelation and asceticism that can make him truly free. At least, I realized that I was no longer supported by anything and that I needed—we needed—to reinvent everything. I wanted to exist in my own right. I loathed nothing more than the contention—endlessly rehashed by my parents—that the meaning of life consisted in sacrificing oneself for one's children. I could only see in this the absurd continuity of the species, an unpleasant stretching out into infinity of the sort that had already made me feel nauseous in my childhood whenever I looked at a box of "Anchor" soap. On each box could be seen a young boy on a large anchor brandishing his own box of Anchor soap, on which a little boy on an anchor brandished ... And so on *ad infinitum*. In much the same way, my parents sacrificed themselves for me, and I in turn was supposed to do the same for my own children, who in their turn would ... I refused to accept this vision of life. Of life as being essentially one vast expanse of seminal fluid that would endlessly be engulfed in nothingness only to be endlessly renewed all over again.

I was wrong, and I was right.

I was wrong because ultimately it is not a question of mere biology but of "faces", and to be of use in the upbringing of a new "face" is for many people their only way of self-transcendence.[37] I was right because, if one expects everything to come from the child himself instead of giving him direction and a sense of life's meaning—preferably by example, silent example—you end by owning him. And your disproportionate love will constrain him and drive him to rebellion. In real paternity there is participation in another kind of transcendence. There is a break with mere biological continuity by the revelation of the love of the Father—a strong sacrificial love that protects and then frees by giving the Spirit. This is why Christ—the Maximum Man, in Nicholas de Cusa's phrase—had to be born of a virgin mother. In order to connect us directly to the Origin; that is, to give us the possibility of a paternity in the Spirit. The death of the father figure, the near-impossibility of being a father today, corresponds to the "death" of God, and the correlative death of man. The hesitation of young people is thus understandable. In my parents' championing of biological continuity, almost as if it were one's fate, there was at least a kind of faith—even if blind and imposed. No

---

[37] The enigma of the human face is a theme that runs through this book as through most of his others. Clément even said to the late Ecumenical Patriarch Athenagoras that one of the reasons he became a Christian was because Christianity seemed to him to be the religion of faces. More importantly, as he wrote in one of his articles, "God himself became a face, and man can now discover his own face and that of his brother". See *Contacts*, 228 (2009), 428.

doubt the day will come when to dare bring a child into the world a genuine, committed faith is precisely what will be necessary.

I may have refused secular morality, then, and the idea of sacrificing oneself for one's children, but I carefully cherished my inherited atheism. In my family, it was in fact turning little by little into indifference. However, my own need to exist—above all to be fully aware of existing—meant that I wanted to give this atheism a basis, to formulate it, to propagate it. I can still see myself at the *lycée* aged about thirteen or fourteen, attacking certain schoolmates who were vaguely Catholic, trying to prove to them that, if they believed in God, it was because they were afraid of death. Poor things, they had nothing to answer me with. We discovered sexuality—that is, the sacred in the raw—and their ill-defined Catholicism wasn't of the sort that could help them resist its appeal.

Eros and Thanatos: it seems to me that the relationship of an adolescent with death is no longer that of a child. Anxiety diminishes. It is the idea of suicide that comes to the fore, though this is above all a way of showing off, death resembling the reflection of Narcissus. True, suicide is sometimes a cry for help. But, at bottom, age is irrelevant; it is always the eternal child who weeps because he is alone.

However, it wasn't in a context of nihilism that my own generation came to know about suicide, as is often the case today. ("I shall kill myself," one often hears, "because life has no meaning.") For although we had used up our spiritual capital, we still felt a certain biological impulse. My grandparents on both sides were of peasant stock and although my maternal grandmother was illiterate, she could count. She needed to! Married to a virile railroad workman, she had given birth to eleven children, nine of whom had survived.

So Eros gained the upper hand over its big sister. I preached atheism and raised my fist for the Popular Front, with a red handkerchief in the breast pocket of my jacket or else sporting on my lapel the badge of the now defunct French Section of the Workers' International. How proud I was the first time I showed myself to my father! He had given a wry smile tinged with sadness.

Eros? Girls and theories ... The erotic use of rationality gives one a feeling of power and peace of mind. Other people are just puppets. But not me, for I belong to the group of initiates who know all about the principles and laws, whether of history, of power, or of libido. For a while, this erotic use of reason becomes the opium enabling one to forget the nothingness. Sometimes for quite a long while. Some old men, for instance, in an attempt to walk backwards towards death, have a transplant of monkey testicles. Or else practise Tantrism, or fine-tune and wield the power of their theories—usually revolutionary theories or ones that deny any idea of transcendence. All in all, however, girls and theories simply serve as planks that can be thrown across the abyss. One climbs onto the planks, plays one's role—for a time. Until that half-hour of silence in heaven that Revelation speaks of (Rev 8:1) and that awaits us all.

Today our intellectual gurus smile with pity whenever one talks of a thirst for the absolute. They inhabit the zone of the relative, indeed are comfortably installed in it. Although not an expert in the matter, it seems to me that I was looking for God even in my very denial of him. And that he was looking for me there too.

As might be imagined, there was no shortage of arguments. At the *lycée* one of the teachers—an outstanding one, by the way—read Sartre's *The Wall* to us. Reductionist philosophies were in the air, thanks perhaps to the rolling mill of the Second World War which had surreptitiously juddered into motion. Times have changed. The student revolution of May 1968 marked the apparent triumph of these reductionist thinkers—and yet their secret, perhaps definitive, failure. For actually it was all mere theatre, not liturgy.

So, the great atheistic "explanations", as I understood them, ran as follows. Marxism is based on social alienation, so evil is simply this alienation, God merely being man's lost essence. Nietzsche stresses the will to power, to health and to creative playfulness. God is nothing more than a word for the illusory world of ideas and values, a refuge for our weakness, and the weapon of our resentment. As for Freud, of course, with his tale of a "super-ego" nurtured by infantile feelings of guilt, God is just the projection of the "castrating father", the sadistic father.

All this—and they say it with an air of superiority—requires lucid analysis, a call for historical responsibility, for justice, creativity, comradeship in struggle and carefree encounters with the opposite sex.

And yet…

All these supposedly lucid people happily tear each other apart so blindly, and know so little how to listen. All these "Gnostics" who think they are "in the know" are in fact rendered ignorant of the pitiful yet beautiful reality of history by dint of hammering it into the confines of their interpretative framework. All these aware people are so unaware in daily life. The relative is inflated with absolutes until it becomes monstrous. Sexual passion, which seems to offer euphoria—"that which I need in order to really exist" — delivers nothing in the end but a puff of nothingness. The path is littered with dead birds.

In 1956, not long after I had been baptized and was slowly learning how to lead a life of humility and forgiveness in which faithfulness becomes possible, I was engaged in a conversation with a young Hungarian revolutionary about the enigmatic meeting of man and woman.

"There is no mystery about it," he said. "Faithfulness is a meaningless shackle."

"All the same, what are your feelings when a relationship, however brief, comes to an end?"

Suddenly his aggressiveness subsided and he reflected for a moment.

"Sometimes," he said, "it's as if I had killed a bird."

Yes, the path is littered with dead birds. One senses that the climax in what is called the act of love is, at bottom, a quest both for the greatest proof that one is alive and for the truth about another human being. Yet it is a quest that misses its two objectives, being unable to harmonize them except perhaps for a few fleeting seconds. A few weeks later, you no longer remember anything — except that song in the dunes hummed by some female or other.

In today's culture the orderliness of a functional, quantitative regime whose machines know nothing of the deep-seated rhythm of life contrasts with the frenzied disorder of the sexual instinct. In order to escape from abstraction and solitude, we are told that we have only our bodies to rely on. However, erotic tension and its release can do nothing but mime the spiritual death that is necessary for the other to exist. Each is in the end simply thrown back onto his or her loneliness. In such cases the thirst for the absolute consists, consciously or otherwise, in expecting everything, for a fleeting moment, to come from another precarious being who also needs saving. Sooner or later the other is ignored, wounded or destroyed. Tristan or Don Juan ... With the latter, the yearning for the absolute is transferred onto pleasure itself, the quest for the sacred onto profanation. It is a case of Narcissus and his reflection once more. But time tarnishes mirrors. They need changing so that one can be loved all over again. And, since everything ends up becoming profane, profanation itself must be intensified. By transgression. At the culmination of such sexual "liberation" loom the actions of the hangman or the slave.

Are these merely the fantasies of certain intellectuals? Perhaps. But there will always be some young people who will try to live—or to die—according to the words of others. I have often thought that the gaze of the Judge on the Last Day would simply be that of a child, calm and a little astonished. A gaze in which each of us will see himself, in which I will see myself. The bringing to light of what we are truly responsible for will be terrible.

Yet a sense of sin is not primarily a feeling of moral culpability. It is more a question of feeling sorrow, of being sorrowful to the point of death. A sadness unto death, says the Apostle.[38]

There also exists a kind of love that is full of this sadness. It is very widespread nowadays.

---

[38] "The sorrow of the world produces death", 2 Cor 7:10.

✢ 2 ✢

War, Politics and Culture

THE WAR THREW ME INTO POLITICAL ACTION. I joined the French Resistance. But total war makes for total politics as well, and anyone who is exacting discovers sooner or later that total politics justifies anything and everything. It justifies lies and violence, with no longer the recognition of any limits—whether what Camus calls a limit of honour or what Solzhenitsyn terms the limit of cannibalism.

We were at war, then. But men of total politics are always at war—a war between reason and chaos. Violence and lies in a surrender to chaos; the sovereign use of violence and lies that their intellect lays claim to. But it isn't true! Violence and lies make us slaves of unknown powers. Blood, to begin with ... A crimson stain is enough. I remember a certain scene in a chivalric romance. A sparrow hawk has swooped down on a defenceless bird. A few beads of blood drip onto the snow. The knight halts and gazes at them for a long time. This "long time" shows that he has become an initiate, it reveals his mysterious vulnerability.[1]

Blood ... I have experienced for myself, during a demonstration, exactly how the sudden appearance of blood opens up a breach into the unseen, causes

---

[1] The allusion is to the verse narrative *Perceval ou le Conte du Graal* by the twelfth-century poet Chrétien de Troyes.

the forces of the nether region suddenly to materialize, induces a bewitchment, a state of hypnosis. It is in precisely such a state of hypnosis that war is conducted. Sometimes it is mere intoxication, sometimes a sacrifice freely chosen. But of this great cup of Wrath,[2] underground warfare is familiar above all with the dregs. Each day brings news of a trap, an arrest, a case of torture, an execution and then a setting off into the mist, into the night. Yet the worst is when the shedding of blood is premeditated, when it is methodically proliferated. In this connection, I recall one such run-of-the-mill instance. We were waiting in a certain hideout when one of the group said: "That Mongol patrol, we can get it massacred—it's being arranged." (We used the term "Mongol" to refer to the auxiliaries enlisted by the Germans from the Asiatic regions of the Soviet Union.)

"Yes, we can," I replied. "But do you realize what reprisals there would be? Remember what has already happened in the village of X, those meat hooks ..."

"But that's the point!"

But that's the point. During those last months of the war, this was something that I could not subscribe to. So I became involved in other forms of resistance. We still risked our lives, but in order to save lives.

I had already discovered that the so-called rationality of the militant was in reality irrational; that he campaigns both in order to escape from himself and in order to find himself; that what keeps him going is not some all-encompassing philosophy but brief moments of genuine, gratuitous communication between friends. Like when I tasted Nescafe for the very first time! It happened in a deserted château

---

[2] Cf. Rev 14:10.

where a few young comrades and myself had met up. In the grounds there was a vast garden and, in this arid countryside where there were practically no trees, its shape formed a clearly identifiable landmark that was suitable for airdrops. One member of the group offered me a cup of this unexpected beverage and it was, as it were, a moment of communion. A few months later, however, we found ourselves on the run at night under the glare of floodlights, and he fell to the ground. You bend down, you see the strangely detached, motionless shape, the bit of froth on the lips, but you've got to move on, got to get running again. The Nescafe may have been a form of communion, but only on this side of death.

✢

Marx says nothing about death. He only speaks of it once—in his *Economic and Philosophic Manuscripts of 1844*—simply noting that "the particular individual is only a particular species-being, and as such mortal."[3] A paltry sort of viaticum!

I remember clearly the day on which I knew I would not become a communist. I had been reading Marx in the university library of a town in the south,[4] discreetly concealing the book under the three hefty tomes of Spengler's *Decline of the West* which I had occasionally been leafing through. Then suddenly something occurred to me, woke me up. Something which spread from my guts to my heart, finally reaching my head. "Pretext." The word preyed on my mind: "Pretext.

---

[3] Translation by Martin Milligan, done in 1959 for Progress Publishers, Moscow. The text is available online at www.marxists.org.
[4] Montpellier.

It's all a pretext!" Things started to become clearer. I wasn't reading this book for what it was saying—about capital gain, infrastructure, praxis and so on. All of this interested me, of course, but it was a pretext. The desire growing within me to join the Party was also a pretext. There was something else. I was seeking something else through all that.

After this quietly tentative Overture came the full blast of the orchestra.

First of all, what about Marx himself? Surely his own state of consciousness must itself have been a reflection of economic and social evolution. Where, then, was the critical distance that enabled him to become aware of this evolution? If, like everyone else, he was alienated, how and on what basis did he know that man had become a stranger to himself? From Neolithic times, moreover. From the first division of labour. There is no God, but Marx's consciousness is apparently absolute, a paper god. And matter just happens to be crammed with its own god-like properties. Matter, history—it seems it is all the same thing. Then again, these people talk of justice all the time, but how did they arrive at the actual concept of justice? Where did it come from? From the evolution of matter? Pull the other one!

Pretexts, pretexts ... But for what?

Some sort of meaning, perhaps. Not one provided by history or evolution. Anyway, I fail to see how a higher state can emerge from a lower. The ascent of life? But why? Yes, the sea may rise, but this is because it is subject to the pull of the moon and the sun.

A meaning for me, a meaning for you. For both of us together. And there, perhaps, you have history. The meaning of collective existence, but through and by means of personal existence with all that this entails of justice, love, beauty and death. Not that personal existence can be separated from collective existence, but the relationship between them is reversed. And each person—who is admittedly inseparable from all—is unique, becomes open to ... To what? I could as yet give no answer, but the question had been asked.

❖

I must admit that the young communists and sympathizers whom I met in the Resistance did not have closed minds. They were in no sense extremist or dogmatic. Mostly they were simple men from the Languedoc who lived close to the earth and who, like myself, were Mediterranean pagans. I don't mean the intellectuals. And yet many of them too lived according to a religion of the sun.

I remember in particular one tough comrade. He was a broad-shouldered, broad-faced man who came from a long line of woodcutters. In times past, these folk had lived a nomadic life, moving from the Limousin region to the Montagne Noire, and from there to Catalonia in Spain.[5] His greatest pleasure seemed to consist in driving our lorries. Yet in his friendship with me he revealed a sensitive side to his character. It was 1944 and I was reading him excerpts from that great book by Vladimir Lossky—*The Mystical Theology of the Eastern Church*—whilst at the same time trying to explain it to myself, for at the time I didn't understand much of it.[6] Whenever the text talked about "God beyond

---

[5] The Montagne Noire is not a mountain, but rather an entire mountain range in central southern France. It lies south-west of the Massif Central, where the Limousin region is situated.

[6] This is all the more remarkable in that the book—on quite a specialized topic—had only been published that same year. Why had Clément bought it? It seems certain that his attention had been caught by the words "mystical" and "Eastern" in

God"[7] and especially about the divine energies that permeate all things, the eyes of this woodcutter, this communist member of the Resistance, would brim with tears. "That's it," he would say. "That's exactly it!"

I also remember a certain factory worker who had become an intellectual, well versed in dialectics. He had got his education from the Party and his Trade Union and had been taught to explain everything on the basis of social background, class psychology and historical context. He was a Parisian with what we called a "clipped" accent. For a long time he had known nothing but town life, the factory and political struggle. The explanations he had been given had worked reasonably well. But, thanks to the paid holidays that had recently been introduced by the Popular Front, a breach had been opened.[8] Along with other young workers he had gone camping in the woods. Every evening they would light a fire. Sitting round it, they had learned how to be silent and, for the first time in their lives, had seen the stars. In Paris the constellations are hidden or muddied by reddish-brown clouds. But now, up above, they came streaming across the night sky as if to eat out of their hands. The sky too was a forest! Some of the workers had been unaware that the moon changed size, waxing or waning

the title since, as he later tells us, this was a period in which he was exploring the religions and philosophy of India and the Far East. See Chapter 4.

[7] That is, beyond all attempts to "capture" God in human concepts—an allusion to Lossky's stress on apophatic theology and to the term *hypertheos*, as used by such Greek Fathers as St Maximus the Confessor.

[8] From 1936 to 1937 the Government was led by this enlightened alliance of left-wing movements (including the French Communist Party). For the first time ever, workers were granted two weeks' paid annual leave.

from one quarter to the other. For them, it had simply been a silly round object, vaguely obscene. But now it livened up their holiday with its changing appearance—although their paid leave did not last for a full lunar cycle. Far from it!

Silence ... the fire ... the night with its stars ... his fellow beings looked at in this new setting ... The effect it had on him was significant. He had never noticed before how a girl's eyelashes would flutter in the wind, or how her smile blended in with the moonlight. No longer did he feel the urge to kill birds. You simply let them land on your hand. They stayed or flew off again, just as they wished. From then on, the old explanations explained nothing. Even when back in the city, they couldn't explain everything. Previously, when faced with a given historical situation, he had known how to explain things, what to expect. But now, looking at people in the way he had learned to do round the camp fire, he could no longer second-guess anything. The unknown—so many unknowns—had entered his destiny.

I believe that today [1975] there are many "communists" of this kind in the Third World. (I don't know about the Far East.) The earth, sunshine, the assistance given to oppressed ethnic groups and as a result the discovery of non-Western culture—bit by bit it all eats away at the enclosed, totalitarian character of Marxism, that product of nineteenth-century Western rationality. Just as it is eroded, for many young people in the West, by the end of a Promethean approach to things, by their respect for the balance of nature, by the realization that mankind is not alone on the planet, and that our duty is not one of mere domination.

Instead of being afraid or worried about betraying their faith, shouldn't Christians strive on the one hand to "secularize" Marxism, to well and truly "demythologize" it; and, on the other, work towards inserting into the context of a divine-human dynamism all this religion of the sun, this religion of unbounded fraternal existence which is seeking itself in contemporary Communism and at the same time contradicting itself? Shouldn't Christians strive to place Marx's specifically scientific contribution within the context of a far more sophisticated and open-minded rationality. Not simply denounce Marxism's "pseudo-religion" but rather transfigure what is genuinely "religious" about it into a divine-humanity that would at last take seriously that great affirmation of the Greek Fathers: God became man so that man might become god.[9]

If such an attempt were one day to take shape, we must be clear about *who* made it possible: the thousands, the tens of thousands, the hundreds of thousands of martyrs that Christianity has known in the twentieth century. Above all—though not exclusively—among the Orthodox. All of them victims of an anti-theistic Marxism. Put to death whilst praying for their executioners.

❖

So I took a different path; I discovered culture. Too avidly, though, to be able to appreciate or even recognize its subtleties, its refinements or its precious subdivisions. At the *lycée* I had been too ill prepared, too unsophisticated and at the same time too demanding to be interested in the literature and philosophy that I was taught. The inopportune response I had given

---

[9] Expressed thus, it is an affirmation found for the first time in St Irenaeus (*Against Heresies*, V).

at primary school to the question of the cold days of November was followed by a similar incident in my French classes. We had to explain how we saw our future. I had replied that I couldn't care less about anything—except to be able live by the sea, close to its vastness. In philosophy lessons it was worse.[10] When the time came for us to write the usual dissertation on the meaning and purpose of this subject, I had contented myself with giving an ironic commentary on the following Gospel saying: "What will it profit a man if he gains the whole world, and loses his own soul?" Which proves, by the way, that I was already reading the Bible. I don't know when I started.

It was only poetry that moved me deeply. From Baudelaire to Rilke, to Milosz and T. S. Eliot,[11] a route mapped itself out, one which led me on a spiritual journey. Dadaism I rejected with a shrug of the shoulders: why should one angrily set about dismantling the language? We should challenge such people as these, who have nothing to say. Surrealism attracted me, but disappointed me. It was a parody of a mystery that as yet I could put no name to, though I couldn't tolerate people playing about with it.

Along with poetry, there was history.

For a long time it had aroused in me enthusiasm, but also horror. One particular school lesson is still fresh in my mind. I am about nine or ten years old. I have just learned that Charlemagne died in 814. Suddenly I feel dizzy: Charlemagne is dead, they're all dead, this

---

[10] Philosophy and the history of philosophy has traditionally been a compulsory subject during one's final years in a French *lycée*, and still is.
[11] The Milosz in question is Oscar, not Czeslaw, his distant cousin, who is better known in the English-speaking world.

book talks only about dead people! Yet I wish to get to know them. Why? It is as if they are in me, and I in them. Louis XVI was guillotined on 21 January 1793. I am the king, hands tied, purposefully mounting the scaffold as I go to my death, and I am also the executioner throwing clots of blood over the crowd.

Shortly afterwards my father gave me a book that fed my imagination for years. It subsequently went missing and I have never been able to track down its bibliographical details. It contained long extracts from the great epics, especially the Iliad, the Ramayana and some passages from the Bible. A sense of the tragic entered me then and has remained with me, with the result that any conception that does not take account of it leaves me disinterested. Old Priam at the feet of Achilles and then weeping over the dead body of Hector ... The abduction of Sita, beloved wife of Rama ... The inevitable, paradoxical death of the daughter of Jeptha ... Samson triumphing at the cost of his own life. Ah, I understand all too well! How I love Dostoevsky who, when a child, wept as he listened to the Book of Job being read to him!

So I became definitively immunized against contemporary hedonism, against the pleasure principle, the eroticization of life, against the idea that self-fulfilment and self-enrichment can be achieved simply by means of lyrical passion. Achilles' lament for Patrocles, Priam's for Hector, Rama's for Sita, Job's cries of rebellion—for me they all mingle with the lament of my mother over the bodies of two of her sisters who were struck down prematurely, the closest ones, the ones she loved most. The threnody of this de-Christianized woman from the Cévennes—who had nonetheless been influenced by the good Book—seemed to be intensified by the angry mutterings of that "stiff-necked" people to whom Job belonged, and by the ancient, raucous cursing against fate.

Both my grandfather and my father had never stopped talking to me about history. About the saga of the vine, phylloxera, the slump in sales, the events of 1907, all those people who had become nomadic supplicants following that unrecognized Gandhi, Marcelin Albert.[12] Above all about the First World War. I would cycle off with my father on what were real pilgrimages, to meet some of his old comrades in arms. They were often indifferent to begin with, it is true, but once we had had a drink together tongues were loosened.

However, what I expected from history was something else. Something other than history in the standard sense. Probably a challenging of the so-called self-evident truths which were stifling me. Probably a concrete manifestation of the total-humanity of each person that I was beginning to sense.[13] Probably traces of eternity.

It was at that time, as a university student, that I made the acquaintance of Alphonse Dupront. He was

[12] See pages 8 and 9 above. Marcelin Albert was the leader of the rebelling wine-growers. The adjective "nomadic" alludes to the many peaceful marches that he led over long distances, in order to gather support and to plead before parliamentary representatives. He is still a local hero, having a college named after him.

[13] Cf. the discussion of Leroux's ideas on page 18 above. As regards his childhood dizzy spell during the lesson about Charlemagne, he had already referred to this three years earlier in *Questions sur l'homme* (Paris: Stock, 1972), translated as *On Human Being* by Jeremy Hummerstone (London: New City, 2000). In doing so, he also provides a clearer answer as to why he should have been so interested in his favourite subject: "history, in the end, is the destiny of humanity with God, and our God is the God not of the dead but of the living" (*On Human Being*, 45).

my first mentor, the person who first taught me how to deepen my understanding of things. Since then he has forged a brilliant career, becoming President of the Paris-Sorbonne University. With his infrequent but extremely dense writings that display an all-devouring intelligence, he has established himself as the pioneer in France of historical psychoanalysis and religious anthropology. (His studies on the Crusades are an exemplary illustration of his work.) Back then, he was a young teacher who had just returned from Romania, where he had spent some years as Director of the Institut Français; for he had a vocation to serve, as he was to show by his work on the fringes of the Resistance.[14]

As well as being one of his students for a while, I also became one of the collaborators in his ventures into spiritual resistance. This was something towards which the disillusionment I had met with elsewhere was pushing me.

For Dupront, any depth in existence is essentially religious in nature. Long before Foucault[15] — who,

[14] The distinguished French historian and anthropologist Alphonse Dupront (1905–90) was an associate professor at the University of Montpellier when Clément was his student there. His major work was *Le Mythe de Croisade*. In 1956 he became a professor at the Sorbonne and in 1960 also became a *directeur d'études* at the École pratique des hautes études, specializing in the collective psychology and the history of European civilization. In the reform of university structures subsequent to the student rebellion of May 1968, he became the first chancellor of the Université Paris IV–Sorbonne. Dupront also founded the Centre d'anthropologie religieuse européenne at the École des hautes études en sciences sociales and was its director from 1972 to 1990.

[15] Michel Foucault (1926–84) was a very different kind of historian and philosopher, whose world-view was far from being religious. Associated with the structuralist and poststructuralist movements, he was fashionable at the time

besides, limited himself to the most recent stratifications of Western civilization—he saw history as being a succession of "languages" and structures, as mental archaeology. Dupront went further. For him, in the final analysis history is never anything but religion or the denial of religion, in the widest sense of the word—that is, people's links with each other and with being. When studying a given historical period, he would begin by examining its semantics. Considering human beings in all their complexity—which also means in all their transparency—he would hold together all aspects and dimensions of their existence in a state of tension (but not necessarily of opposition), no one of them being considered determining. Compared to dialectical materialism, this was for me a definitive liberation—not by a side-stepping of history, but by approaching it more scientifically.

However, like Jung, Dupront did not go beyond the immanent. Whether something else was contained in the immanent or whether immanence was closed in on itself, who could say? Which is why I left him a few years later. Because of the tragic aspect of life, because of the living God. He set me free from not a few limitations and gave me the courage to go my own way, which is what he wanted.

There was something else about him. He was a fine gentleman. Noble and simple—two words which are almost identical. A gentleman of the intellect, in the way he used his creative powers, in the way he wel-

---

Clément was writing. He is mentioned here on account of his trans-disciplinary approach and, in particular, his so-called "archaeological" method. The word figures in the subtitle of his 1966 book translated as *The Order of Things: An Archaeology of the Human Sciences*.

comed you. A "Captain of Gascony", bright-eyed and fair-haired, who functioned at full capacity.[16]

He often stayed deep in the Armagnac countryside, on a small estate in a zone that had already been liberated. The prefecture had been peppered by German machine guns. When I went there I would stroll about arrogantly. Sometimes I crossed paths with the commanding officer of the place—me with my juvenile recklessness, he with his strangely detached air. Leaving the town, he would walk peacefully by the riverside of an evening, accompanied by his one aide-de-camp, completely unprotected. We often looked at each other. I was wearing leggings and riding breeches. It was ridiculous, but I wanted to show that I too was a combatant. A few kilometres outside town, you came across the outposts of the Maquis,[17] a few men in blue overalls carrying old rifles. And then, dusty and taciturn, I would arrive at Dupront's place. The large room was like a cool cistern. There was a jug of water handy. Then he would take me across fields in which

---

[16] Gascony is an area (a pre-Revolutionary province) in southwest France, covering several modern regions and departments, including the region of Aquitaine that Clément refers to later. Dupront came from this part of France. The particular phrase *cadet de Gascogne* alludes to the historical fact that in the seventeenth century the "Captains of Gascony" were a French regiment under Louis XIII. They were mainly recruited from the youngest sons (the "cadets") of the aristocratic families of Gascony. For them it was the only way of acquiring fortune and glory. The regiment was considered romantic and swashbuckling, so it appealed to authors. It figures in Rostand's play *Cyrano de Bergerac* and in the original *Three Musketeers* by Dumas. Despite Dumas's fictionalization, a person called D'Artagnan actually existed.

[17] Dense shrub land proliferating in the Mediterranean region; the term is used as the nickname for the guerrilla bands of the French Resistance, who hid in this terrain.

the corn was higher than we were, through woods in which he would march straight ahead, whatever the obstacles. The light in Aquitaine is like liquid gold. It has the resplendence of Mediterranean light but with more body. He loved walking. A nervous disorder — one that he had calmly mastered — had caused him to become acutely aware of the physical sensation of the act of walking, of really feeling the ground beneath his feet, with a sort of gratitude. It was while we were walking that he would question me. About whom I had met, what stage we were up to with such-and-such a matter, a contact established, a prisoner freed, supplies moved up the line, a task force or an official assignment organized.

As I watched this man live, act, come up with new ideas or solutions, and influence all those around him, a problem presented itself that I had never thought about before. The problem of nobility and perhaps wisdom, too. It had nothing to do with class struggle or class psychology. My grandfather was noble, despite being a simple peasant. And this important academic — who at the time was on the fringes of society, engaged in a fight for the future of France and the whole of Europe, a lasting future, indeed a spiritual one[18] — he too was noble. Henri Michaux once said that a country in which the girls are pretty is a good country.[19] One

[18] Further insight into what Clément and Dupront believed they were fighting for is provided by the following remarks: "It wasn't primarily the Republic that we were defending, but France. We were as if organically attached to the independence of the Kingdom of France, as we often called it. A kingdom without a king." *Mémoires d'espérance* (Paris: Desclée de Brouwer, 2000), 19.

[19] Michaux (1899–1984) was a poet, essayist and painter, who often linked his images to his texts. The remark is found in *Passages* (1950), a collection of various poetic texts — the one in

might also say that a civilization in which those in charge are morally noble is not such a bad one either. (As for the hereditary nobility, well "today everyone is bourgeois", as Péguy said long ago.[20]) It is a problem that we have too often overlooked, but one that Dupront and Dunoyer de Segonzac (whose activities were similar in nature) were discussing at the time in writings that circulated clandestinely, often being copied by hand.[21]

Nowadays everyone talks about power, but *never* about the people who exercise it. Towards the end of his life, Lenin discovered that Stalin was uncouth. Ontologically uncouth, one might say. The Revolution was over, the Party was in power, but the General Secretary of the Party was uncouth to the point of being inhuman. Somewhat late in the day, Lenin discovered the problem of a person's moral value, and also that culture cannot be subdivided. There isn't one culture called "bourgeois" and another called "proletarian". He discovered that morality cannot be divided either. Rather late, in truth. Neither nobility nor wisdom

---

question being "Visages de jeunes filles", written after a visit to China.

[20] In his 1913 essay *L'Argent*.

[21] Pierre Dunoyer de Segonzac (1906–68) was a distinguished army captain who fought heroically at the head of his troops against heavy odds until the defeat of France in 1940. In September of that year he became the director of a new institution whose aim was to train the elites that France would need. It was based in a château at Uriage-les-Bains near Grenoble. Its relative isolation allowed him to exercise considerable independence and Uriage became a breeding ground for the Resistance. Not surprisingly, two years later the Laval government closed the place down. At this point he and his team became full-time underground activists in the Resistance. Shortly afterwards, he became Maquis commander of an entire region, his network comprising Catholics, Protestants and Jews.

can be achieved by decree. There are rules. Time is required. Sources of inspiration are needed. I had learned that there exist men whose authority compels recognition without coercion or, if it coerces, does so without humiliation. Men who know how to prune trees, in particular the tree of history. Can there be the beginnings of communion in any society without the recognized presence of such men?

✣

My discovery of culture also included art and science and, thanks to Dupront, getting to know men who were dedicated to one or the other.

In the creative act—when after a long, patient process something is set ablaze (or perhaps, especially when one is young, an angel of fire pays a sudden unexpected visit)—beauty torments us with an insatiable nostalgia, fleetingly conveying a plenitude that offers a presentiment of something else. In the convulsive explorations of contemporary artists, it seems as though—suppressed by a civilization that is too superficial—a cry is struggling to burst forth from the depths of their being. A cry in which artistic calling, revolt, intoxication and celebration are all rolled into one. Yet there are other artists—more reserved, more industrious, following in the footsteps of the Romanesque sculptors and of Poussin, Chardin and Cézanne—who little by little draw back the veil that hides the mystery contained in the visible, the mystery that I had paid homage to as a child. Its Face and Name remain in the beyond.[22] However, God was undoubtedly making his

---

[22] Reversing the order of the nouns, Clément used this same phrase—"Le Nom et le Visage"—as the title of an article that first appeared in *Contacts*, 186 (1999). It was reprinted in *Sillons*

way towards me by means of works of art like these, such as those paintings by Manessier[23] in which night settles around a face that is never actually depicted. There was Braque too, and Bazaine.[24] I hadn't yet met Lorris Junec—an artist who, with serene yet as it were nuptial passion, knows how to reveal the very being of things. Their paschal being.[25]

Science can or may eventually be able to explain everything—save for this cry, this imperceptible groan, this radiant patience. Yet perhaps in its own way science too points to transcendence. It too can become celebration. I was one of those who, during and after the Second World War, considered Simone Weil to be far more important than Jean-Paul Sartre. She often reflected on the contemplative dimension of science, on science as one possible dimension of a culture of attentiveness. If scientists delve deeply enough, she says, they are struck by beauty, for the scientist's "true

    de lumière (Troyes: Éditions Fates, 2002), a collection of his texts on beauty and art.
[23] Alfred Manessier (1911–93)—a non-figurative painter, stained glass artist and tapestry designer—was much influenced by his stay in a Trappist monastery and by the relationship of the monks with nature.
[24] Jean Bazaine (1904–2001) was a writer as well as a painter and, perhaps more famously, a designer of stained glass windows.
[25] Lorris Junec (1899–1993) was a Croatian, born in Zagreb, but from 1925 he lived permanently in Provence and obtained French nationality. He and Clément became close friends. Clément kept one of his paintings in his study (see *Mémoires*, 11.) He also devoted an important article to him, one in which he discusses more widely the spirituality of such paintings as his: "Terre: À propos d'une exposition de Lorris Junec", reprinted in *Le Visage intérieur*, 259–67.

aim is the union of his own mind with the mysterious wisdom eternally inscribed in the universe".[26]

The ancient Cistercian abbey of Sénanque is today a cultural centre. Its director, Emmanuel Muheim—a man of deep thought and poetry—is a friend of mine.[27] As a way of introducing visitors to the sober beauty of the cloister and the church, he first makes them pass through a room on whose walls he has arranged blown-up "scientific" photos in which the rhythms of the nebulae and the structure of minerals or organisms prove to be temples, to be theophanies. The "systems" that form what out of habit we call "matter" reveal an intelligence that astounds the onlooker. Yes, which grips one at the core by its beauty and wisdom. Sometimes Emmanuel mingles with the visitors or else takes over the duty of the guides, who are themselves veritable initiators. Before these images, and surrounded by the "negative theology" of the archi-

---

[26] Simone Weil, *The Need for Roots: Prelude to a Declaration of Duties towards Mankind*, trans. Arthur Wills with a preface by T. S. Eliot (London & New York: Routledge & Keegan Paul, 1952), 256. Reprinted in the Routledge Classics series in 2002.

[27] Emmanuel Muheim (1923–2002), poet and essayist, had also been a member of the Resistance. By 1969 there remained only five monks at the twelfth-century abbey of Sénanque (near the village of Gordes in Provence). It had become impossible for them to continue. Fortunately, a wealthy industrialist who wished to establish a cultural centre had been looking for a suitable site. Having signed a thirty-year lease agreement, he undertook the restoration of the complex of buildings in collaboration with the Ministry of Culture. The monks moved to the abbey of Lérins, the mother house on Saint-Honorat, one of the islands of Lérins (a place associated with Vincent of Lérins and also John Cassian). From 1970 to 1988 (the period Clément is describing) the place was a thriving centre of cultural activities of the highest standard. In 1988 a community of monks returned from Lérins, and Sénanque became once again a Cistercian abbey.

tecture, no-one can remain unmoved. Here and there under the photos Emmanuel places a quotation from the Bible or the Fathers, so as to reveal the cosmic face of Christ—"For in him were all things created, in the heavens and upon the earth".[28] The ordinary folk who visit are often deeply affected. The Knights of Nothingness, on the other hand, armour-plated by their reductionist explanations ("It's just ... it's just ... and *I know!*") receive a blow to their self-esteem and often break out in curses. "Whoever did that deserves to be shot!" one of them exclaimed one day. These are the lukewarm that the living God "spews out".[29]

At the time I am talking about—during the Second World War—I myself could doubtless have been described as one of those whom the Book of Revelation refers to as torn between cold and heat. (Yet cold burns, too.) As an adolescent, I had read widely about astronomy, evolution and scientific cosmologies. This was during the holidays, when I was back in the village. There I would recreate just for myself the old rite of the fire at dusk. After grandfather's death and the encroachment of urban manners, this particular custom had fallen into disuse. What I am about to say might provoke a smile, but I wanted the villagers to retain above all an intuitive feeling for these customs, yet not an artificial if knowledgeable display of them. And if intuition also raises a smile, well, so be it!

In cosmology I had been struck by a concept that, so it seems to me, is being verified more and more—that of a *beginning*. So this much-vaunted matter is not eternal and this beginning, I said to myself, is not *in* time; it is the beginning of time. Time and space

---

[28] Col 1:16.
[29] Rev 3:16.

might not then be undefined *containers* forming a prison without walls but from which we are nonetheless unable to escape. I was also struck by the fact that Einstein pointed out the relativity of space. Not only does everything spread from an initial point, but this "everything" is itself "curved" and thus *contained*. On this same subject, right in the middle of the war, I was deeply touched by the meditations of Milosz who seems, by purely spiritual means, to have had a *vision* of relativity long before Einstein. It is the movement of my fall, he says, which makes of space-time an infinite prison where I am detained, pathetically shivering in the gloom. But "the totality of space, within which thought is manifested, appears to us not as something which contains, but as the illuminated interior of the beautiful crystal that is the Cosmos, fallen from the hands of God."[30]

I must admit that, even when I was devising the most virulent form of atheism, the various theories of evolution always seemed to me absurd. I wanted to subscribe to them, but couldn't. I wanted to believe I had descended from a monkey—or rather from a common ancestor—but found the whole business foolish. Later I came across Soloviev's witticism, made about the young revolutionaries of his time. Here is their slogan, he said: "Man is descended from the monkey, so let us love one another." This was precisely what I could not bring myself to say. (Incidentally, the

---

[30] From Oscar Milosz's cosmological prose poem *Psaume de la réintégration* (1925). Milosz was a French Lithuanian poet, metaphysician and diplomat. His highly personal and dense Christian cosmology has been compared to that of Dante and Milton. The Orthodox writer and translator Philip Sherrard devoted an article to him, "Oskar Milosz and the vision of the cosmos", *Temenos*, 6 (1985), 284–97.

revolutionary students of Paris in May 1968 were much more logical with their "Let us love *on* one another." When Soloviev was alive, no-one had thought of coining such a saying. The Russian revolutionaries of his day were chaste.)

What! Homer, the Ramayana, the Bible, my beloved epics, the tears of Priam, the faithfulness of Sita, the faith of Job—was all this supposed to have been produced by the restlessness of an amoeba that had become strangely complex by the blindest of chance? One must be insane to believe such things! I could discern design and continuity in the appearance of living forms. But, because of the perfection and infinite complexity of each of them, I also saw their radical discontinuity. It is a point of view that seems to have been confirmed by recent discoveries in genetics. In my case it originated, no doubt, in my Mediterranean astonishment at the luminous plenitude of each thing. Whether one likes it or not, the gaze of every child of the Mediterranean is Eleatic,[31] indeed Platonic. God is a designer. One has to be crudely northern to imagine, as did Jung when a child, that he merely does his business on the world. In fact, all lyrical accounts of evolution—including those of Teilhard de Chardin, whose writings I read

---

[31] The Eleatics were a pre-Socratic school of philosophers who influenced later Platonic metaphysics. Clément is here alluding to that aspect of their thought which emphasized the difference between appearance and reality, since information obtained by the senses is illusory. They were opposed to the theories of the early physicalist philosophers, who explained all existence in terms of matter. Although the adjective "Eleatic" is rarely used by Clément, we do find time and again in this book as in his many other writings a phrase (or a variant of it) which points to the same idea: "le secret dans l'évidence"—that is, in what *seems* obvious or self-evident.

in typescript during the war—made me think of this divine defecation.

You people don't know how to be amazed, I thought, or how to wonder at the humblest of living beings whose incredible complexity is incorporated within such intelligent and beautiful *limits*! I see now that the very form of things has always been for me an opening onto transcendence.

One must positively wish to be an atheist when the very design of creation—with its continuities and discontinuities as clear one as the other—point to, indeed demonstrate, intelligence. True, there was a darker, more obscure, side to things; namely, that so much wisdom and beauty should be intermingled with death even if, admittedly, it were woven into the fabric of the universe with a master's touch. Like everyone, and for a long time to come, I also came up against the problem of evil. Faced with a universal order that seemed far too complicit in horror, I gave up. I did not yet know that original Wisdom is shot through with the tragic (that which is within myself first of all); I did not yet know that, driven out of his creation, the Creator could only have regained entry as the Crucified One; I did not yet know that the power of the Resurrection requires man's freely given co-operation for the universe to be perfected and transfigured. However, I was making progress. Isn't the mistake, I thought, to view the world simply from the outside, "back to front" as it were? Thanks to my historical studies, I was considering other cosmologies, medieval and oriental. (Under a pseudonym, I even wrote an article on alchemical cosmology for a special number of the *Cahiers du Sud*. Today, in translation, it is enjoying success in the United States and apparently helping young seekers after God to discover Christianity by a quite different route!) I had begun to sense that there was a connection between things of a kind different from the "horizontal" ones underlying the process of so-called evolution. An inner connection.[32]

Nowadays some American scientists believe that the structures of matter derive from "realms of consciousness" that participate in a common Source. Already for Einstein the very intelligibility of the universe implied an "It knows". These scientists compare this Source to a set of programmed patterns, which makes me think of the *Logos*, the Word, and the *logoi* of the things he created—their "words" or essences, or intelligible principles—so often referred to by the Greek Fathers. Or else they compare it to a "mother language" that all humans try to speak, each in their own way. And that makes me think of the Word "in [whom] all things were created", a principle dear to the powerfully cosmic theology of the first centuries. St Maximus the Confessor maintained that the perception of even the simplest of things constituted a Trinitarian experience: its very being relates to the Source of being, the Father; its intelligibility, to the Word who is Wisdom; and its moving towards plenitude, to the life-giving Breath, the Spirit.

---

[32] For this lengthy artcle he used the pseudonym Maurice Aniane, Maurice being his middle name, Aniane the name of the village where he was born. "Notes sur l'alchémie: 'Yoga' cosmologique de la chrétienté médiéval" first appeared in 1953 in a volume edited by Jacques Masui entitled *Yoga, science de l'homme intégral* (Marseille & Paris: Éditions des Cahiers du Sud). The book contained over twenty essays by various authorities, such as Mircea Eliade. Interestingly, Clément's own text is immediately preceded by "L'Hésychasme: yoga chrétien?" written by Metropolitan Anthony (Bloom) of Sourozh. The article was later included, along with two others by Clément, in a small volume entitled *L'Œil de feu* (Fontfroide-le-Haut: Éditions

Fata Morgana, 1994; reprinted by Éditions de Corlevour, 2012). Clément wrote this text in the period leading up to his baptism and reception into the Orthodox Church (November 1952), when he was still searching among the world's religions and myths for the truth, being dissatisfied with Western Christianity's a-cosmic stance. Yet despite its title—which sounds somewhat "unorthodox"—he never disowned it, as is evidenced by his agreeing to its republication some forty years later in *L'Œil de feu*. Significantly, however, in this book he sandwiched it between two more obviously Orthodox essays in a way that demonstrates the progress of his thought. In the specially written introductory text—entitled "Éros et cosmos: révolte ou assumption"—he gives some account of how it was Western alchemy's concern with "transmutation" that led him to Orthodoxy's belief in "transfiguration". He has in mind the original aim of the alchemists, which was to purify, mature and perfect materials. It is important to note that the word *yoga* in the title of the article which occasioned this footnote is in inverted commas, for Clément is concerned with the term's etymological and metaphysical meaning: joining, union, integration. A few citations from the article will demonstrate just how it already contains phrases and lexis that will pervade all of Clément's further writings. Alchemy at its purest, he writes, was "an immense effort to awaken man to the divine omnipresence"; to see that things are permeated with the "divine energies"; to see that nature can become "transparent"; that "the 'eye of the heart' can see gold in lead and crystal in the mountain because it can see the world in God". The true alchemist attempted "to help nature, suffocated by human decadence, to breathe the presence of God", and to offer up to him "the prayer of the universe". Alchemy was also "a logic of integration" in that the cosmos is viewed as being "an immense Anthropos". The closing essay is a masterly summary of the Orthodox view of these things, and that amply demonstrates the full development of Clément's thinking. Entitled "Transfigurer l'univers (le cosmos dans la mystique de l'orient chrétien)", it is a rewritten, expanded version of a text that first appeared in *Contacts* in 1967.

✢ 3 ✢

Death and Other Enigmas

My introduction to politics and culture exposed me once again to the fundamental things. Anxiety once more, wonder again. And now, faces as well.

Confronted with death, its anguish and loneliness—especially spiritual death, of which our biological end is merely a sign—people today are perhaps more defenceless than ever before. It seems that our civilization is the first in history to do all it can to brush death aside, and in so doing perhaps discloses its very essence. Funeral rites are expedited as quickly as possible, or else disappear altogether. People no longer know what to say, what to do. When I was a child, even in a milieu that had for long been bereft of any Christian frame of reference, nobody was ever left to die in a hospital. When there was no longer any hope, the sick person was brought home and surrounded with more affection than ever. A vigil was kept, not just whilst the person was dying but also after they had died. It was almost unbearable, since it took place in the face of nothingness. No-one prayed. Who would they have prayed to? And with what words? No-one read the Psalms or the Gospels. They no longer even rounded things off with one of those crudely restorative funeral meals. We were no longer in Christian territory, everything had been forgotten: the living God, the soul, the resurrection. But yet it wasn't paganism either. For according to this, one dies impersonally in vegetal manner, peacefully fading away into the vast beyond, becoming a seed, passing on to the other side of things until the next sowing season. No, what had still been retained from biblical revelation was the certainty that this dead person was unique and that his or her life was theirs alone.

These wakes were characterized by naked anxiety. You went to the kitchen for a cup of coffee and then came back to sit by the corpse again. In silence. Always that silence. True, people busied themselves, over-meticulously, with the usual things that have to be seen to after a death: the announcements, the funeral arrangements, the family tomb and whether one should gather together the dust of the earlier occupants so as to make room. Tombs that were in cemeteries without crosses. Anyway, for most people the cross no longer signifies victory over death, but just a cemetery. So, like any good rationalist, one might as well avoid such tautology. Without crosses, then, but with the well-constructed heavy slabs typical of Mediterranean cemeteries. Family pride was important, so it was felt that plots should be reserved "in perpetuity". Then there was secular rationalism's obsession with cleanliness, which meant that the relatives would pull out every last blade of grass. It also explains why the municipality has got rid of all the pines and cypresses. Not that this prevents the soil—which is too geologically recent in the low-lying, vast plain where the cemetery is situated—from sinking a little, nor the slabs from collapsing. They tip over, like in those scenes of the Last Judgment depicted on Gothic tympana. My daughter cheerfully hums the *Dies irae*. They teach it her at school in history of music lessons.

Nowadays, in similar milieus, the dying are left to pass away alone. Either they are in hospital and stay there, or else, if they are at home, the rest of the household goes off to bed. Because everything has been done. Because there is nothing else one can do. The dead person is left alone in the bedroom until, as quickly as possible, they are removed. People no longer know what people everywhere have always known, whatever their understanding of death: that in reality no-one dies alone, that the love and prayers of the living make the final exodus easier. In America there are corpses plastered in make-up, in the Soviet Union cemeteries that are abandoned—it is all evidence of the selfsame state of affairs. In France, people of my generation have seen an entirely secular Day of the Dead become established, indeed become over-developed. One day in the year is devoted to the dead, just as Polycrates threw his ring into the sea to ward off bad luck.[1] It is a cult devoid of hope and one that has completely overtaken All Saints' Day. A ring for the sea, chrysanthemums for death. "I, Death, continue to reign!"[2]

[1] According to the historian Herodotus, Polycrates (tyrant of Samos in the sixth century BC) was so fortunate in everything he did that his friend Amasis (ruler of Egypt), who feared that such unprecedented good luck boded ill, advised him to part with something which he highly prized in order to escape a reversal of fortune. Following this advice, Polycrates threw a valuable jewel-encrusted ring into the sea. A few days later, however, a fisherman caught a large fish and decided to offer it to the tyrant. As Polycrates' cooks were preparing the fish, they discovered the ring inside it. Amasis now renounced his friendship with Polycrates, considering him to be a man doomed by the gods. Not long afterwards, in fact, Polycrates was killed by his host, the satrap Oroetes.

[2] In Europe the relatively recent "secular" Day of the Dead is officially 2 November (like the religious feast of All Souls'

In order to forget ... to forget ... people seek to satisfy humanity's one fundamental desire—its yearning for eternity—by means of consumption, eroticism or politics. True, life is celebrated. One's pregnant partner, for example, is photographed in the nude—a pomegranate with a single seed—but the child to be born will be born to die, and its life on this side of death will in effect be eaten away by death. Because physical death cuts short—and at the same time mysteriously alleviates—a certain spiritual state, a certain condition of existence. One that is characterized by separation and failure, by opacity and a state akin to sleep-walking, by a heart both hardened yet fragmented, by an intelligence which opposes or else confounds, and by the myriad shimmerings of pride and despair.

Standing in a large Parisian cemetery over a deep, narrow grave that is reinforced with technical know-how, a man bursts into heavy sobs. The coffin seemed to go down and down for ever. Five minutes later, he is busy with his affairs again. A funeral is an affair, too. He chats, he has forgotten. Death is a thin fissure, quickly closed up again. It is no longer anything, but contaminates and spoils everything. Nietzsche's Madman, after announcing the death of God and the reign of nothingness, calls for lustrums and feasts. They will be of a kind unheard of, he says. And so they were. One need only recall the concentration-camp regimes

---

Day, which it copies). Yet in many if not most continental European countries it is All Saints' Day on 1 November that is a public holiday. Thus in recent decades many people have anticipated things and adopted the tradition of visiting family graves on 1 November, the "wrong" day. In France and other European countries, they typically take chrysanthemums, these having long been associated in these parts of Europe with bereavement and death.

of the first half of the twentieth century. These too, for some, were permanent feasts. In fact, any world view that does not take death into account can only be a murderous illusion. It ends in the death of others, or in a state of commercially orchestrated sleep-walking. Each lives as if he or she alone were not going to die. How many prepare for the transparency that is possible in old age? "When I am no longer capable of making love," one hears it said, "I shall kill myself!"

The transparency possible in old age ... There are certain stages in life that have no meaning unless they are seen as an overture to transcendence. Childhood, for example, that is so tormented by limitations. Or any state of faithfulness—whether to one's spouse or to one's vows of virginity—that deciphers the face of the other in God, that recognizes in Christ the face of God. But above all, old age. Will one escape the segregation that threatens and the isolation that has already begun? Will one be surrounded by tenderness and a diverse mix of ages and conditions in a rediscovered community life? If death is not accepted and transfigured, old age has no meaning. This is what old age needs: meaning. Not a mechanical prolonging in which death is forestalled without being internalized. Only a trusting resignation to the fact of one's death—to a death the fear of which has been removed by Love—can give grand old age its power of benediction, its gratuitousness and its connivance with childhood. Otherwise one risks becoming spitefully jealous of the youth of others, or nursing a pettiness that trades the fundamental anguish for minor cares and obsessions. Or else there is that long silent suffering, that hidden despair, those discreet suicides that are committed since life is petering out anyway and since one hasn't found, in the Breath come from elsewhere, a second wind, a new lease of life. A contemporary writer recently killed himself because he was no longer able to see. In ancient Greece, however—as is still often the case today in the Third World—the greatest poets were themselves blind, yet they were seers![3] Old age facilitates a different kind of knowledge, the kind the Christian East sees as resulting from the union of the mind and the heart. The changes that take place in old age can even be measured scientifically. There is the loss of neurons, certainly; a striking reduction in their number; but also a prodigious enlargement of those that remain and that should from now on function *differently*.

So childhood and old age form, as it were, a circle of iridescent transcendence around the torments, passions and struggles of middle age. The civilization of nothingness has broken this circle, notably by positing sexual life as the only normal expression of the *eros* that can legitimately be discerned both in the child and the old person. The spiritual death of the father brings in its wake those of the child and the grandfather.[4] The archetypal wise old man or woman is no longer found, no longer has a place in family or social life. Adolescents lose their zest for living—except in the frenzy of some short-lived paroxysm—since no-one shows them an example of true fulfilment in life. Then, when they reach the age of forty or fifty, the frantic struggle to prove one's efficiency at work means that they miss out on the learning process of another kind of knowledge,

---

[3] The contemporary writer in question was presumably Henry de Montherlant, who committed suicide in September 1972 (when Clément would already have begun to write this book). In a note left behind, he wrote: "I am going blind, so I am killing myself".

[4] An allusion to Freud's so-called "father complex".

that of the soul. Even should they try, society would punish them with economic death.

What I like about the Christian East—which cares little for fashion—is the respect and admiration shown to old people. A man who has set out on the path of spiritual learning is called a "noble old man", whatever his actual age. And, here, beauty is not separate from wisdom or love; it rises from the heart. Look at the old monks of Athos or Moldavia whom age has set free. They exhibit a reserve which might seem to be affected, but which is in reality the cocoon of the chrysalis. The lips become refined and drawn in, the forehead broadens and acquires a pearly sheen, the whiteness of the hair and beard bear witness to a transfiguration, the eyes regain the solemn wonder of childhood—though they shine less, yet communicate a calmness that is beyond all passion and all fear. The very flesh of their hands becomes dry, light and pure, like that of a small child.

All things considered, my grandfather and my aunt from the village were "noble old folk", too. My aunt's only regret was that she hadn't been allowed to die during a serious illness when, already very old, she had sensed that the moment had arrived and had peacefully prepared herself. They cured her, prolonged her life by a few years, but she lost her independence and in the end, to some extent, her head. As I have already described, my grandfather and aunt were supported by an entire culture. Nor were its sources in the remote past. A culture, a hard-won wisdom. When I was a child, those women in the village who were more than forty or fifty years old would dress all in black, obliterating their bodies in long dresses. They became just faces. A hard-won wisdom ... Bones are hard, too; but it is their marrow that nourishes the blood.

It was not until later when I had become aware of the reality of the resurrection and had got to know the Christian East (though I now know that the West—above all in its monasteries—has its own secret Easts) that I would again meet any radiant old people. People whose mere presence helps you to live, to die, to transform yourself by the remembrance of death. Such a one was Patriarch Athenagoras, who was over eighty years old when I first knew him.[5] He was a person of benediction; young people were not mistaken in sensing this. He was possessed of a childlike capacity for wonder. As seen in the way, in February, he would greet the first tree to flower in the garden of the Patriarchate, or in how he would spend ages watching the patterns made by birds against the sky from Marmara to the Golden Horn, or by ants on the ground. A wise man's detachment made him able to listen, to welcome, to dive into what he called the "inner ocean of a gaze". He no longer had any fear; anxiety had changed into trust. He had received the gift of prophecy. He knew, since Christ is risen, that any historical situation, however tragic, can be creative, a time of new birth. He knew, for instance, that it was the very angst of the West that meant that, from now on, it was here that must take place the annunciation and example of what the resurrection means, of life stronger than death.

When the time came, he knew he was about to die. His friend Metropolitan Meliton talked of a journey to Vienna for a surgical operation. "No," he had replied. "It is for another journey that I must prepare myself".

---

[5] In 1969 Clément wrote a book, almost 600 pages in length, entitled *Dialogues avec le Patriarche Athénagoras*. Despite what one occasionally reads, it has never been translated into English.

He received holy communion and then refused all food. He thanked everyone and asked to be left alone. That is how he died, in that one-to-One encounter in which one is no longer separated from anything.

In the spring of 1974 I was in Romania, giving a course of lectures in the theological institutes of Bucharest and Sibiu. I discovered that many peasants there prepare their own coffin in advance, and live on intimate terms with it. There was nothing gloomy or tense about these preparations, made whilst they were still enjoying good health. They waited for death as for a marriage, with Christ as Bridegroom, the sun and moon as groomsmen, and the stars an abundance of lighted candles.

I visited the monastery of Cernica, near Bucharest. In the middle of a lake on a plain, two islands are joined by a causeway. The Romanian monks have had a gift for choosing initiatory sites. On one of the islands is the monastery, on the other a church and a cemetery. As in Russia, and already in Central Europe, there are no heavy slabs or funereal monuments. Just a cross, most often of wood, and some earth. A little mound from which flowers burst forth.

> And flowers rise from the earth
> That are like the forgiveness of the dead.[6]

Cuckoos call. Acacias sag under the weight of their white bunches of flowers in which bees buzz. I remember how much I loved acacias as a child. When the first summer winds came, it seemed to me as though they were laughing.

---

[6] From "Cantique du printemps" by Oscar Milosz, included in his *Poèmes: 1895–1927* (Paris: Fourcade, 1929).

Several local friends accompanied me, and each insisted on showing me his own grave. Everything is ready: the name, the date of birth. The only thing lacking is the date of death. They tell me they often come here to this cemetery to reflect, to meditate—amid the fragrance of the acacias, the song of the cuckoos and, not far away, the prayer of the monks. In the Christian East a monk is someone who wishes to enter death alive, to become a person of resurrection already here below. Among those who walked with me that evening in May, it seemed to me that there were two such "resurrected" people. (We all are, but they were consciously so, with a transforming awareness.) People whose death would not be an agony but a simple "falling asleep" in which one passes to the other side of things and continues to serve Love. One of the two, a sturdy building contractor, was the more talkative. The other said almost nothing, but just to be close to him caused one's heart to melt with an ineffable sweetness.

But I am getting ahead of myself. I haven't been able to avoid discussing important opinions and certainties that are mine today. Besides, what I have just written about the way death is treated in our society is no longer altogether true. When the time comes during which great tenderness is required—all the greater for being devoid of hope—people will draw closer together and console each other like timid orphans. They will accompany each other towards death, tenderly. Certain researches in the field of thanatology are paving the way for this. It will be the subtlest form of atheism. One will die in an ecstasy of love—facilitated by means of the appropriate drugs—surrounded by attentive friends, and consummating very gently an incestuous relationship with nothingness. But all the same Christ will be close at hand and perhaps, before this comes to pass, Christians will have rediscovered the paths of resurrection.

What I wanted above all to recall—to remind myself of—is that during and after the war I had refused to shy away from the fact of death, from the enigma of our mortal condition. The sunny immanence of youth was already beginning to fade. This light was round about me, but not within me. On the few rare occasions in my childhood when, for short periods, I had left the Mediterranean region, everything had seemed black and slimy. The light that occasionally came to rest on things was, as it were, alien, something extraneous. An extrinsic grace, in the sense understood by Protestant theology! Near the Mediterranean, on the other hand, the light is at the very heart of things. Today I would compare this to the Orthodox conception of grace. As for Catholics, they know the light is there but, to be safe, have preferred to depict it in their own way, with all the colours of Thomistic logic. They even call it *created* grace!

Yet little by little I discovered that even in the full light of the South, it is human beings who can still be black and slimy. Myself, first of all. The light is at the heart of *things*, but not necessarily of persons. Or perhaps it is simply that persons are far from their own hearts. I began to orchestrate situations in which I could find self-fulfilment: at the Student Services Centre, sometimes a position of authority over a few people, the use of my creative gifts, and the irresponsible games of love. Then suddenly, in broad daylight, the sun ceased to shine and everything became extrinsic to everything else. It took a long time for me to discover that I was not merely sad, but guilty; not merely hurt and separated, but someone who himself caused hurt and separation.

Going to live in Paris facilitated the necessary self-examination. I remember going for long walks in the former "zone" which had been turned into garbage dumps and waste plots, though it was not yet covered with rows of low-rise buildings and high-rise blocks of apartments.[7] On certain days in autumn large butterflies with heavy wings flew over this urban steppe-land. The next day they were gone. I would walk faster and faster, then suddenly sit down and stretch myself out, tortured by an asphyxia that was not just spiritual. I could no longer breathe. Not even inwardly, with that fundamental pulsation of which physical respiration is merely an echo. In order to be able to breathe again, it seemed to me that I would need to progress beyond a certain dimensionless point, to break through an iron doorway against which my teeth clashed. The Gospels speak of the eye of a needle, through which the rich cannot pass.

I have seen many people die. Death is also a mystical state that pacifies and, as it were, a blessing that reveals one's true face, one of supernatural beauty. I have often had dreams about death masks, though I don't much care for photographs. (All those people who want to "take" a snap with their cameras! The truly sensitive photographers who know how to reveal things are few and far between.) All the same, when at the age of sixty-one my father died—quickly, discreetly, still

---

[7] The Paris *zone*—short for non-building zone—was originally part of a military defence system built around the city's fortifications in the 1840s. A narrow strip of semi-rural land, its main function was to facilitate the visibility of approaching enemies. In the early twentieth century, around the time of the war, poor people began to set up shanty towns there. Since the mid-1970s, the word has been associated with the troubled housing estates on the outskirts of Paris, to which Clément's sentence alludes with its "not yet".

silent—I did get a photographer to come, so as to capture his transfigured face. I still have the photo. It was taken a little too late, when earth had already begun to return to earth and yet it retains the imprint of that other sun.

I remember, too, a young man who died of a generalized cancer. He was a member of one of the discussion groups I had organized in about 1950 and whose investigations were conducted on the borderline between politics and the spiritual. The questions that had awkwardly been raised, along with certain other factors, had at least helped him become aware of his Jewishness. He had made a start, at least. A gifted mathematician, he had begun to read Spinoza. His illness came out of the blue, striking him down like a stunned beast that didn't understand what was happening. I kept vigil by his side in the hospital on the university campus and was able to witness the changing appearance of his face. It had been a round, open face, and he had worn round spectacles. He had a look and a smile in which lively intelligence was mingled with humour. But now all roundness had disappeared. All the Parisian intelligence had gone. What suddenly took its place, sculpted by suffering, was the sharp face of a desert nomad. The face of Isaac as the knife glinted above him. The God of Spinoza had disappeared, being replaced by the God of the night and of destitution. The young man became engulfed in this presence, or rather this searing absence. After his death, his parents—who were indifferent from the religious point of view—stuck to their secularist principles and decided they wanted him to be cremated. A few of his fellow Jews and some friends, including myself, gathered in the Parc Montsouris as close as possible to the spot where the hearse would pass. When it came into view, the ritual prayers were intoned: "May his soul be bound up in the bond of life eternal." The sky was low, it was raining a little.

✣

Faces ... Where do they come from? This flesh that is at times permeated with a light not that of the sun. Breeches in the ill-defined prison walls of this world. Leading to what secrets? As a child I loved the faces of the old peasants, that ancient cracked clay that was already dissolving in the water from their eyes. Faces of patience and sorrow such as I no longer see nowadays save among the immigrant workers from Portugal or the Kabyle who wander bewildered in our cities. Cities in which even the familiar faces look worn out—though never completely so—by meaninglessness and nervous exhaustion, by a habit of haste that turns time into an enemy rather than an ally. Pebbles swept along in a human torrent, caught up in a mechanical process of wear and tear, marked by a type of suffering new to human history—one that no longer remains below the surface but is clear for all to see. The women may be beautiful, but this is often thanks to an impersonal mask through which their voices sound false. Yet there still are the beautiful faces of children, especially when asleep or when paying close attention to something, and occasionally, as I have already suggested, the face of a dead person. When all is said and done, each and every face is of value, however stricken by individual or collective destiny and regardless of the scars of however many failures, however many troubles. Every face is a cross, on which the person is engendered. Even if turned to stone, a face is flint from which a spark can still fly.

So, faces are an irruption into matter of ... of what? If nothing exists apart from matter, what are they? How can the vibrating air emerging from a mouth touch one's heart, cause the eyes to shine, or create a presence. What is this secret space in which we speak and think, this depth which is common to us all, this centre where we meet? Yes, why are there faces at all, if everything emerges from nothingness only to return to it?

✤

And so, despite the various ideologies with which I had become acquainted, within me was rekindled the wonderment of childhood. Moreover, the mystery of faces seemed inseparable from that of things. Do you remember what happened one winter's evening to Rubin in Solzhenitsyn's *The First Circle*? He was an ardent communist, but in this scene we are far beyond ideology and politics. He has been radically challenged by several violent moral shocks, then one night he goes outside into the prison yard and suddenly feels "the innocent, child-like touch of cold snowflakes on his beard and flushed face". He stops, closes his eyes and is "enveloped by a delicious sense of peace. This powerful sense of being was all the keener for being so short-lived. What happiness it would be if he didn't have to go anywhere and beg for things, if he had no desires at all but could just stand here like this the whole night, as blissfully as the trees there, catching the snowflakes as they came down."[8] Things have become freed from banality, from being taken for granted. They open up like embers cleared of their ashes by the wind, moving beyond our grasp. Seized by the joy of simply

---

[8] Alexander Solzhenitsyn, *The First Circle*, trans. Michael Guybon (London: William Collins & Harvill Press, 1968), 508.

being alive, Rubin "scooped up a large handful of the gleaming white floss [...] and filled his mouth with it. He felt as though his soul had partaken of the freshness of the world".[9] When unmasked in this way, being is perceived to be transparent. But transparent to what?

As may already have been guessed, it was then that I had a first revelation. Not yet a conversion, but the discovery of another country, the invisible dimension of the visible for whose exploration the whole of eternity is required. Not yet a conversion to Christ—though I did discover him too, though without knowing what to make of him—but a discovery of the soul and of the infinite. Professional theologians who happen to read these lines will most likely turn up their noses. They don't like "religion". And so they have manufactured for us an empty faith and, ultimately, an atheistic Jesus who turns out to be just an incarnation of man. These people, who were taught about God in childhood (badly, no doubt, but … well, I have said the word "badly" so let's move on), these people simply do not understand that someone who grew up in an atheistic setting, someone shaped by atheism in his entire being not just his way of thinking must first of all experience a revelation of the invisible, of the spiritual—of the as yet anonymous Spirit. If not, he is unable to even understand anything of what Jesus says about himself. Let us leave this quarrel on one side. I don't pretend that my personal journey is exemplary. Others will please you more. But allow me to think that religion is the content of faith and that everything is religion, even the rejection of religion.

And so I discovered the multiform infinity that flows through the whole of human history, constituting the

---

[9] Ibid., 509.

lifeblood of its noblest creations. As a historian myself, I perused with a sort of euphoria the *musée imaginaire* of revelations, of Revelation.[10] "The very stones will cry out", said Jesus to those who asked him to silence the children who acclaimed him as he entered Jerusalem. Today the children have indeed been silenced, and the stones do cry out. I hold a stone in my hand and it cries silently of the suffering and the joy of God. Of a God who speaks and is at the same time silent, causing it to exist. I walk along the seashore with a salty pebble in my mouth, and my silent mouth cries out of God.

I enter the Romanesque church of Saint-Guilhem-le-Désert and experience God's silence.[11] Human architecture such as this is needed in order to create this silence, for in nature even the most barren landscape

---

[10] For information regarding Clément's main career (i.e. as a teacher of history), see the Introduction.

[11] This famous abbey (which gives its name to the small medieval village which grew up around it) is but a few kilometres from Aniane, the village where Clément was born. It nestles in a dramatic landscape of gorges and waterfalls. Guilhem was a cousin of Charlemagne. As Count of Toulouse and Duke of Aquitaine, he was entrusted with the task of pacifying and defending the area against the Saracens. He was renowned as one of the most valiant warriors of his time, his exploits becoming celebrated in medieval ballads of knightly prowess and chivalry such as the *Chanson de Guillaume*. In 804, however, having befriended St Benedict, he decided to found a monastery. Two years later he himself became a monk there at the age of 48. Wishing to forget the style of life he had led in the world, he stuck to performing the humblest of tasks in the garden and kitchen, taking part in the offices as a simple monk. He fasted and spent entire nights in prayer. It was after his death in 812 that the abbey was renamed in his honour. The present building—a jewel of Romanesque art and classified by UNESCO as a world heritage site—dates from the eleventh century. Part of its cloister is in the Cloisters Collection of New York's Metropolitan Museum of Art.

crackles with a thousand noises. As I go further into the church, the space becomes, as it were, incarnated. I go down into the crypt and the redoubled silence becomes my origin and my end. No longer signifying nothingness, it cures me from having been born only to die. Back in the nave, I go forward into the glorious body of the building, into this embodied presence, towards the apse and its blessing. For there, high up in the thick walls of the clerestory, a cross has been cut out between two ocular windows. A cross of light between the moon and the sun, as these windows are nicknamed.[12] For me at that time, the cross signified invisible transcendence (symbolized by the vertical bar) breaking into the visible (symbolized by the horizontal). I didn't yet know what price God had to pay—and still pays—in order to reintroduce this transparency into our flesh.

Back outside again, I walk in the wind high above the church towards a natural amphitheatre, known locally as the End of the World. It is as if a cosmic nave and apse had been carved into the limestone mass. The tall, towering cliffs stand for God's severity, the olive trees lower down the slopes his free-flowing gentleness. The sky is like a cupola and now, along with the open sky, I can say Yes. I climb to the top of one of the cliffs and lie on my back, letting its vastness—this transparent abyss, this blue fire—enter my being.

I enter a North African mosque, barefoot and silent. I visit former mosques in Spain. Although these are not places of incarnation, they do contain a void that is so pure, so noble. And a kind of poignancy that dissolves all heavy sadness, being a confirmation of the intangible. Curves everywhere—over doorways, in the arches,

---

[12] A photo of this impressive feature can be seen at http://www.art-roman.net/saintguilhem/saintguilhem4x.jpg.

the arabesques and the inscriptions. Curves that never close around a central point but that intertwine and multiply in an attempt to capture him. But always he slips away ... Him, him!

It wasn't yet the Word of God; but his silence. A silence in which things come together, are pacified, open up. A silence of plenitude and nostalgia, in which one's thoughts find free space and in which one can at last breathe, get one's breath, pass beyond the stage of asphyxia that I had been experiencing in the urban desert of Paris where butterflies fluttered over garbage. Air at last, being able to breathe at last. Then another kind of respiration opened up inside me. I had always known about it, I had always known but they had always kept it hidden from me. They all hide it, those who uphold this civilization of the void, just as do those who struggle against it. But God exists! You only need listen to the stones. You only need listen to those countless people down the ages who have glorified his unpronounceable Name—*nomen innominabile, nomen omninominabile!*[13]—the saints, the prophets, the humble creators of love and beauty, those who ceaselessly weave on a fleshly web a thread of eternity that prevents the fabric from tearing. Witnesses from the West and from the East. Those whom God fills with his radiance, those whom he consumes with his absence. Those who go out into the deserts and whose pure holocaust frees the world from asphyxia. Those who sit down at the table of sinners to embody the infinite in an act of love. Those who built, painted and sculpted

---

[13] The expression is Meister Eckhart's. Clément elsewhere suggests the following translation: "The Name that cannot be named, the Name that is named by all things". See *L'Œil de feu*, 79.

Chartres, Ajanta and Borobudur so as to embody the infinite in beauty. As I was soon to read in Berdyaev: "The main argument for the existence of God lies in man himself, and in his vocation. The world has known prophets, apostles, martyrs, heroes, contemplatives, seekers after the truth, selfless servants of truth, creators of beauty, themselves beautiful, people of great depth and spiritually powerful. And above all those who have borne witness to the fact that the only truly hierarchical situation existing in this world is that in which one is crucified for the truth. None of this proves anything, but it allows one to discover God."[14]

God exists, which is why we are able to speak to each other with patience and respect. He is the centre to which all lines converge. In him fell asleep and were awakened my father and Charlemagne. In him, in his voluntary absence—for he is a secret call not an external fact—all history evolves, whether it seeks him or rejects him. In him we are no longer separated from one another. From him comes the light of faces that, in a manner of speaking, are "not made with human hands" (as is said of certain icons), being "born, not of blood, nor of the will of the flesh, nor of the will of man, but of God".[15] In him the being of the world finds its incandescence. He is the limitless space of our freedom. Without him we would merely be paltry particles of the universe and of history. Bubbles on the surface of nothingness, amoebas grown complex by chance, uttering an insane laugh on the threshold of death—the laugh of a madman. But he is the bow, the arrow and the target; the beginning, the middle and the end; the centre and the circumference; or rather

---

[14] The source of this quotation has so far not been identified.
[15] Jn 1:13.

the non-localized, the always beyond and yet the place where we are. For he is entirely other and yet more us than we are ourselves.

> The person blind to the One is utterly blind to everything; but he who sees in the One contemplates all things [...] Being in the One he sees all things; and being in all things he sees nothing. The person who sees in the One perceives through the One both himself and all men and all things.[16]

✥

There followed several months of exhilaration and some definitive clearings out.

The great reductionists and atheists have been unable to get to the heart of things. At the heart of things there is horror, but also the pulsation of the Spirit. At the heart of man there is horror, but also the image of eternity. He who does not find gold in the sieve of his science is using a sieve whose holes are not fine enough.[17] The true Yes to the earth is not that of Nietzsche, but Dostoevsky. Nietzsche's Yes seeks to affirm life but what he calls "life" is mingled with death, is a carrier of death. The dancing divinity wears a necklace made of a thousand heads, as the twentieth century has reminded us. Dostoevsky experienced similar temptations. As Berdyaev put it, "He knew all that Nietzsche was to know, but with something

---

[16] Symeon the New Theologian, "One Hundred and Fifty-Three Practical and Theological Texts", §35, in *The Philokalia*, vol. 4, ed. and trans. G. E. H. Palmer, Philip Sherrard and Kallistos Ware (London: Faber & Faber, 1995), 31.

[17] The imagery is more telling in French, since the word used here for "sieve" —*cible*— also means "scrutiny", "analysis".

added".[18] Something added ... Remember the wedding at Cana, when the Infinite sets the earth ablaze, transforming primal water—which is also, after all, the banal water of everyday life—into mystical wine. For true mysticism is nothing other than the ability to perceive the extraordinary nature of the ordinary.

A certain chapter in *The Brothers Karamazov* comes to mind—the one entitled, appropriately enough, "Cana of Galilee." The *starets* Zossima has just died. Impertinent even in death, he allows himself to give off an obnoxious smell just like every other dead person, instead of the odour of sanctity that the pious were expecting. Devastated, his disciple Alyosha nevertheless keeps vigil by his corpse whilst a monk reads St John's Gospel. In a sort of dream, Alyosha hears the account of the wedding at Cana and he sees ... He sees the *starets* seated at the nuptial table near the Solar Bridegroom, beckoning him to join them—for all are called—and the wine of eternal gladness is brought. When he wakes again, the young man goes out into the garden. The night sky is like a vineyard of stars that are harvested by the domes of the cathedral, from where wine flows down onto the world. Overcome with joy, Alyosha throws himself onto the earth, kisses it, and discovers it to be a form of eucharistic communion. When he rises again, he has become an adult, capable of witnessing and of being creative.

Anyone who has experienced such an embrace of the earth is liberated from the "masters of suspicion".[19]

---

[18] N. Berdyaev, *Dostoevsky: An Interpretation*, trans. D. Attwater (London: Sheed & Ward, 1934), 62.

[19] A phrase coined by the philosopher Paul Ricoeur in a book published in 1966, translated as *Freud and Philosophy: An Essay in Interpretation* (1970). The three "masters" are Marx, Nietzsche and Freud. "All three", Clément explains elsewhere, "called

I realized that claiming to "explain" the Gospels, or the Upanishad, Lao Tzu or Master Eckhart on the basis of economic or social infrastructure (like Marx), or on the will for power (like Nietzsche), or the avatars of the libido (like Freud)—well, it was not serious. It was simply the pretentiousness of sophisticated ignoramuses who had been trapped in the strait-jacket of two centuries of Western history. I rejected nothing of the earth, but I had discovered the weighty importance of heaven.

It also occurred to me that the understanding of man found in the writings of the great atheists—which is penetrating but one-sided—should become for us a means of ascesis.[20] It should help us understand, not truth, beauty or love—which come from elsewhere—but their bestial-human disfiguration, the way they are misused out of social fear, class hatred, jealous weakness and resentment. And also in the tragedy of sexuality. Then the transition—one that Nietzsche himself sometimes wished for—from a merely "moral"

> into question the authenticity of our discourse, *suspecting* it of being full of convenient lies" (*Mémoires*, 103). An entire section of *Mémoires* ("Accueillir les maîtres du soupçon", 103–21) is devoted to a Christian response to these thinkers, one that at the same time discerns what is important about them.

[20] In 1966 Clément had written an article on this very theme for *Contacts*. An English translation was published the following year in *Sobornost*. See "Purification by Atheism", *Sobornost*, Spring 1967, 232–48. Also relevant is "Jean-Paul Sartre ou l'affrontement de l'athéisme et du nihilisme", in *Les Visionnaires: Essai sur le dépassement du nihilisme* (Paris: Desclée de Brouwer, 1986). It is also included in O. Clément, *Une saison en literature*, ed. F. Damour (Paris: Desclée de Brouwer, 2013), along with a similar article on Camus. In a similar vein is "Dionysos et le ressuscité: Essai de réponse chrétienne à l'athéisme contemporain", in *Évangile et révolution* (Paris: Centurion, 1968).

God to a God who was truly "divine" would become easier. Seen in this way, as part and parcel of a renewed asceticism, the masters of suspicion are able to inspire a "negative" or apophatic approach to God and to man. I began to like Sartre, for instance, when I discovered that he was the inheritor of an entire Christian tradition of asceticism,[21] and that deep down he was in search of personhood and freedom. It is true that with him "remembrance of death" never becomes "remembrance of God". He gets out of it by focusing on revolution. But here again my mistrust surfaced: "It is just a pretext!"

A monk is mistaken if he believes himself to be asexual—perhaps he intends to say something else—but Plato is more profound than Freud when he sees in *eros* a thirst for immortality, of which sexual life is not the only expression, nor the highest.

Marx never reflected on the Indo-European tripartite division of society, which seems to imply that there have always existed several complementary types of socio-cultural vocation, and that contemplation (together with all thinking nourished by it) as well as a conscious, limited, wise exercise of authority are just as important as production.[22] When, in Marx's fascination with a supposed original absence of class differentiation, Shafarevich detects a regression, a death

---

[21] An allusion to Sartre's austere Protestant background.
[22] Clément is referring to the theory of the French philologist and social anthropologist Georges Dumézil, according to which most Indo-European tribes maintained a tripartite division of societal functions that was reflected in their organization, ideology and mythology. The three divisions were sovereignty (priests and judges or administrators), martial (warriors to protect society) and economic (farmers, craftsmen and tradesmen). Marx based his analysis on a much simpler twofold division.

instinct, he exaggerates. But the problem is worth posing.²³ At the time of my discovery of the spiritual, a friend who had followed a similar path came out with the following quip: "Marx? It's Hegel, as read by a *shudra*", *shudras* being precisely the socio-cultural class that reduces everything to a question of production.²⁴ Whereas what is needed, so far as is possible influenced by contemplation, is a transformation of production into creation. This is no pretentious, demiurgic proposal—man fashioning himself and his universe—but one that argues in favour of a truly nuptial collaboration between man and God that makes use of all the flesh of the world.

Freud's theory of a pleasure principle, with its crude lyricism of self-fulfilment, is shattered each time anyone decides to sacrifice options and possibilities that are perhaps brilliant in order to throw themselves into the fire, becoming in the process an anonymous witness of that fire. But it is then that the angel stays Abraham's arm, that Job regains his wealth, and that Symeon the New Theologian and John of the Cross write their poems. However, in the act of leaping one does not know the outcome and perhaps never will, at least here below. But who would dare to say that the destiny of a Simone Weil was a failure just because, instead of a life of self-indulgence, she chose—even to the point of dying from it—one of communion with those hungry for bread and meaning?²⁵ Conversely,

---

²³ Igor Shafarevich (b. 1923), a renowned mathematician, was also an important dissident during the Soviet regime. He wrote several books and articles that criticized socialism.

²⁴ A *shudra* is a Hindu of the lowest caste. Typically, they are (or were) labourers or service providers.

²⁵ Simone Weil decided early in life to sacrifice opportunities to have love affairs—deliberately making herself look as

a seemingly insignificant, ordinary individual such as Thérèse of Lisieux, living in an enclosed milieu, is nonetheless able to be freed from every kind of limitation so as to become for evermore the one who intercedes for an assassin condemned to death. The assassin condemned to death that we all are.[26]

> plain as possible—to fully pursue her vocation to improve social conditions for the disadvantaged. In 1934 she took a year's leave of absence from her teaching position to work incognito as a factory labourer, believing this would help her to connect with the working class. Even when she resumed her teaching career, she donated most of her income to political and charitable causes. After a lifelong struggle with frailty and illness, she was diagnosed with tuberculosis in 1943 (whilst working for the French Resistance in London) and told to rest and eat well. However, she refused special treatment and seems to have limited her food intake to what she thought would be the equivalent consumed by the poor in occupied France, often refusing any food at all. She died the same year at the age of 34.

[26] We are all "assassins"—Clément explained elsewhere—in the sense that we "daily murder [Christ's] love"; see *L'Œil de feu*, 93. The actual assassin alluded to above was Henri Pranzini. In the summer of 1887 the newspapers were full of his case. Convicted of the brutal murder of two women and a little girl, he represented all that threatened the decent way of life in France. Thérèse, aged 15 at the time, prayed hard for his conversion throughout July and August. Yet Pranzini showed absolutely no sign of remorse. However, at the end of August the papers reported that, just as his neck was being put in place on the guillotine, he had suddenly grabbed the priest's crucifix and kissed it three times. Thérèse was overjoyed and believed that this was a sign that her prayers had been answered. By "enclosed milieu" Clément means the Carmelite convent in Lisieux, though at the time Thérèse had not yet entered, having been refused on account of her young age. However, eight months later the authorities, worn down by her strong-willed insistence, gave in and she was allowed to become a postulant. Yet Clément's comment is not incorrect, since Thérèse continued to pray for Pranzini after his death throughout her life. Indeed, she understood that her vocation

included devoting her life to praying for all sinners, identifying with them. It is to this that Clément alluded a few pages earlier, when he referred—without mentioning her by name—to Thérèse's commitment to imitating Jesus (see Mt 9:10–11) and sitting at what she called "the table of sinners". He refers to this expression of hers time and again in his writings. It may surprise some readers to learn that Thérèse has always been highly regarded by many Russian Orthodox—including Paul Evdokimov, Vladimir Lossky and Fr Alexander Men, who kept a photo of her on his desk. It seems that—after St Francis of Assisi—she is the best-known Western saint in Russia. Many priests admit to having been affected by reading her autobiography (*The Story of a Soul*), which was translated in 1950. In 1999 crowds rushed to venerate her relics as they toured Russia, from the depths of Siberia to Kazakhstan. See Michael Evdokimov, "Sainte Thérèse de Lisieux et saint Silouan de l'Athos: deux saints pour notre temps", *Contacts*, 221 (2008), 47–58.

✢ 4 ✢

The Temptation of the Far East

Getting to the heart of the matter was not easy. Once I had discovered the realm of the Spirit, who was as yet anonymous, I needed to find my bearings. I spent some ten years trying to find my way through this world that my Western, French, Parisian education had concealed from me but that did have quite a few affinities with the Mediterranean intuitions of my childhood. I studied the spirituality of India and the Far East in general, as well as the archaic symbolisms suggested by Simone Weil that René Guenon attempted, somewhat awkwardly, to systematize. I was above all attracted by the precise, perceptive way these things were presented by Mircea Eliade. Yet it seems to me that, more than anything else, it was India that I loved. Long before today's hippies I took the road to Katmandu. Amorous India, at once erotic and sacred! India, land of profusion where everything is reabsorbed into the great silence of negation—*neti, neti*, not this, not this—which is also the omnipresence of a cosmic, feminine divinity. The dark, gentle face of this goddess—Shakti, the divine Energy—reminded me of the face of St Sara, patron of the gypsies, whose statue is in the crypt of the fortress-like church at Les-Saintes-Maries-de-la-Mer.[1]

---

[1] The village of Les-Saintes-Maries-de-la-Mer is on the coast of the Camargue, of which it is the capital, in the Rhone

The crypt, the spring, the saint's dark brown face, and the sacred sensuality of this people come from India: Sara-Shakti.

Immemorial India, that remembers the Origin whenever a woman pours a little milk onto the root of a banyan tree, or whenever of an evening at a stopover place men and beasts bathe together, and where the cow takes on the gentleness of the Mother.[2] The Ganges,

---

delta. It has been a sacred site from as early as Celtic times at least. Tradition says that a group of Jesus' followers were expelled from Palestine some ten years after his resurrection, being put on a boat without sails or rudder; this is the spot where it is said to have ended up. Among those on board were three Marys (Mary Magdalene, Mary Salome and Mary the mother of James). The identity of Sara varies according to the different versions (an Egyptian servant of the Marys; a local woman who helped; the rejected wife of Pilate, who was himself exiled to Gaul according to the Church historian Eusebius), but in all of them she is singled out as being dark-skinned. The statue of her in the church's grotto-like crypt does indeed have a face of gentle beauty. The present medieval church, which is built over and around much earlier constructions, is not only huge but does indeed resemble a fortress. This is due to the frequent raids from the sea by Vikings and, later, by corsairs and Saracens. The church served as a place of refuge for the surrounding population, especially during sieges. The original holy spring, which was now inside the larger building, provided drinking water on such occasions. Sara's skin colour and features have resulted in her becoming the patron saint of the gypsies, whose pilgrimage here in vast numbers has become a major feature in the calendar. Gypsies are believed to have originally come from India, and it is a fact that the gypsies in this part of Europe—especially the women—can look remarkably like Indians.

[2] The banyan is India's national tree. It is considered to be sacred and to be the resting place of the god Krishna. There is an old custom of bringing offerings to it, something reflected in Clément's comment. Furthermore, its own "milk" (sap) has medicinal properties.

that flows down from a divine mountain to the divine sea, is itself divine, as are all the rivers. Amorous India that combines mysticism with eroticism in a fascinatingly ambivalent manner. The world is a place where God plays games, assembling and dismantling things at will. Calculated yet meditative couplings adorn the walls of his temples. As for the yogi, he experiences the body differently, from within, as a bundle of breaths that he frees and unites with the respiration of the universe itself. For India is methodical and technical in opening up paths from within and in building bridges in order to strip away dead skin in her attempt to reach the non-duality of the immutable, universal Self.

India: all is full.

Buddhism: all is empty.

The Buddha demythologized India, retaining only the concept of Awakening. So that he would not escape his princely responsibilities, they built him a palace such as our civilization would like itself to be: a place where one never saw a sick person, an old person or a corpse. But the Law was fulfilled. The over-happy prince did after all come face to face with the enigma of nothingness. As a result, he left his own people, and cut his hair. Not lingering among the proud ascetics, he meditated and became awakened, became enlightened: the world is on fire, burning with desire, and from desire comes suffering. And what is man but an impermanent aggregate that propels itself from existence to existence? There is only the Self, says India. There is No-one, says Buddhism. The sage extinguishes desire, extinguishes suffering, and is awakened to ... to nothingness. He becomes a void, an opening up of infinite compassion to everything and everyone, who are nothing. An opening up of infinite peace to the nothingness that is all.

What moved me most of all was the story of the Buddha's smile, a smile without commentary.[3] Those Zen masters who developed this strand of his teaching prefer humorous aphorisms, naked incoherence—and even the stick—to subtle metaphysics, which Buddhism did also inspire. The silent meaning of this smile spread to Japan, becoming incorporated into the rock and sand gardens there. O those empty beaches of my childhood on which the wind scattered the sand, arranging it into subtle patterns, and where here and there the seabirds wrote indecipherable messages with their feet. Now, they have vandalized you, built meat warehouses all over you. Yet I only need come across a picture of a Zen garden to see you again in my mind's eye as you once were.

Little by little, however, several things began to bother me. Two experiences that for a long time had reinforced each other now began to clash: the experience of being, and that of faces. The Hindu sense of the *supreme identity* versus the European sense of *I* and *Thou*. During the war, I had asked myself what France and the neighbouring countries meant to me, for like many young men of my generation I was not particularly patriotic. The answer seemed to be that they had best expressed themselves in a certain quality in the way the face was represented in art—sober, eschewing the picturesque, almost Jansenistic, as in the portraits from the time of Louis XIII. A certain reality of the other, then. An acceptance of his or her difference, but also the hope of an encounter. The research

[3] Elsewhere, discussing the *logoi* of things, Clément gives a clue as to why this was the aspect of Buddhism that had impressed him. The Buddha's smile when contemplating a flower could almost, he says, be described as expressing a "philokalic" experience; see *L'Œil de feu*, 86.

undertaken by Alphonse Dupront was along these lines, and later I realized that similar things were said by Albert Camus in his *Lettres à un ami allemand* and by Antoine de Saint-Exupéry in *Lettre à un otage*. In short, the tradition of portrait painting seemed to me to be one of the constant features of European art. (I am speaking of Western Europe, for it was only later that I came to know about icons and how they do away with the ambiguities of individualism.) Even the most obnoxious and destructive artists have painted admirable portraits. In each of them an absolutely unique Thou both gives itself and at the same time holds itself back. The barrier is insurmountable but can, if only occasionally, become transparent to the radiance of the inaccessible.

What also epitomized France and the neighbouring countries were certain landscapes. Again, not picturesque ones but landscapes characterized by a beauty that is discrete, born of a thousand-year-old encounter between man and the earth, in which man has worked together with the earth as if to fill it with heaven. A Romanesque church in the Languedoc, for instance. Or one of those ageless sanctuaries in the Île-de-France region with their square, squat bell-towers with buttresses at the corners, releasing the earth's praise. Or simply, on a hillside in Tuscany, the subtle interplay of vines, cypresses and olive trees. These are Christian landscapes, as I was later to discover, in which man does not merge with sacred nature—which is the strong impression one gets when climbing the steps of the Temple of Heaven in Beijing, for example—but ones in which he saves her. Not by "ex-carnation" but "incarnation", by yielding to the materials—as a craftsman would put it—so as to reveal the Wisdom inscribed within.

Faces, materials—I was already far from India. India where, even among the singers of Krishna the God-Love, the person is never identified in absolute terms. The all-consuming experience of non-duality can always be sensed in the background, effacing the *I* and *Thou* in a transpersonal Self. The Self is identified with the divinity in the famous saying: *atman* is *brahman*. But which divinity, I asked myself? There are so many gods, and yet there are none. The image of a bubble, which for a long time had been preying on my mind, presented itself again. Men, the worlds, the gods, God himself—they are all mere bubbles on the surface of the abyss. They emerge from it only to return there. The abyss breathes, sleeps and awakens once again in a cycle stretching over billions and billions of years. Moreover, each year is made up billions of billions of other years. Bubbles inside bubbles. It was worse than the advert for Anchor soap that had so perturbed me in my childhood. And these vast numbers only served one end: to reveal the illusion of the world and the vertigo of time. Ultimately, there is only *brahman, atman,* the Self. It is not for any love of the other that one loves the other, but out of love for the Self, that beloved ogre. Our bodies waste away, fester and die prematurely. An entire people may be reduced to inertia, but all is for the best. Even evil. All is well because all is ambivalent. The world is both a game played by God and at the same time pure illusion. Each of us is born, suffers and dies in his rightful place before beginning the continuous cycle again in keeping with the implacable law of transmigration, in the only hope of one day becoming enlightened to the truth—the truth that in fact nobody transmigrates for there *are* no "persons"! The truth that there is neither "day" nor "knowledge", only the Self. All is replete. All is a paradise. A paradise lost.[4]

✤

Another thing I discovered was that between the various spiritual traditions of mankind there existed insurmountable contradictions.

I felt that René Guenon as well as his disciple Frithjof Schuon—who was perhaps also his rival—and all those who talked serenely of the "transcendent unity of all religions" were getting out of the difficulty somewhat cheaply—or rather, perhaps, at an exorbitant cost. (I met Schuon around that time. Rendered ashen-faced by my juvenile assaults, he had had no answers to my questions and doubts.) Or they were in effect putting themselves in the place of God. Or else they were reducing all spiritual traditions to just one—in their case to that of India, more precisely to the radical non-dualism of the Vedanta tradition. This is what Guenon did with Islam, too. Persuaded that Christianity had lost the "knowledge" (in the sense of a transformative, liberating gnosis), he settled in Egypt after being initiated into Islamic esotericism, but interpreted Sufism from the point of view of a systematized form of Vedanta. His system is slick, though many of those of his followers whom I encountered seemed somewhat schizophrenic.

---

[4] It is interesting to note that when distancing himself from Hinduism and Buddhism in another book, Clément clearly links his thinking to the important theme of the face. "The only thing that counts is this abyss [of love]. It does not have a face: it is an ocean of bliss in which everything is dissolved." See *Taizé: A Meaning to Life* (Chicago: GIA Publications, 1997), 8.

On several occasions I met Hindu "masters", too. Unfortunately, they had become westernized for the worse and in them India had lost all its innocence. They present their "philosophy" in an extremely rationalized form so as to make it suitable for exportation, tailored to a Western market. They have a head for money as well, selling amulets at high prices to rich, dissatisfied American women. As for going to smoke marijuana in Katmandu, what a mockery! In spiritual warfare any recourse to drugs is a sign of failure.

Yet the West is clearly receptive nowadays to the impersonal spirituality of India, and to its yearning to escape from time. India, on the other hand, is becoming open to the demands of historical processes. And already in China, which for so long was influenced by Buddhism, a provincial materialism mixed with puritan activism has become established.

Everywhere, perhaps, a divine-humanity is expectantly awaited, and it may be that this interplay of religious contrasts is preparing the way.

In India, at Benares on the steps going down to the river, corpses are burnt. Smoke rises into the vastness of the sky, ashes fall on the water that ceaselessly flows ever onwards. A fusion with the infinite... Everywhere there are gloomy sanctuaries whose floors are humid and as if magnetized, and where the divine takes all forms—elephant, mouse, the phallic axis of the world. Immanence with its plenitude; immanence with its ambiguities. And then suddenly you come across a mosque, light and empty, infinitely pure, its minaret pointing to the Unique One, who is inaccessible but close at hand. Who is Someone.

Someone... Here you have the naked faith of Abraham, he who set off without knowing where he was going, leaving behind a world of plenty that teemed with animals—just like India—to become a nomad of the Word. The Word that resounded in the secrecy of his surrender, calling to him, conveying a promise, eliciting hope. And so Abraham traded the present moment for history, sacred prostitution for conjugal fidelity, and meditative enstasy for the desert.

It is significant that to this day the only sacrifice recognized and celebrated by Islam, amid the smell of sheep whose throats have been freshly slit, is the one unaccomplished by Abraham. In the Vedas, on the other hand, the most ancient of the Hindu scriptures, everything is a sacrifice. A sacrifice through which the divine becomes immanent. In Islam there are no other sacrifices except for the sacrifice of faith. God writes in Arabic on the tabula rasa of Mohammed's illiterate heart—the God of the desert, of a burning absence, who at every moment creates the world out of nothing. India is spherical, Islam vertical: witness the minaret, the cypress, the finger of the dying person, a single finger raised to indicate transcendence. For it is neither a question of loving God nor of becoming saturated with plenitude, but simply of bearing witness.

I got along quite well with the extreme monism of Ibn Arabi and Persian mysticism, in which the divine is dissolved in an efflorescence of angels and lights. But I still kept stumbling against the God of the Bible, and the Jewish people.

God speaks, the Living One calls: *I–Thou*. He desires man's freely given faithfulness. History is freed from cycles. God chooses. He does not choose India, but a stiff-necked people. Not one immersed in the divine, but someone come face to face with Someone, struggling with him until dawn.

This allusion to Jacob's struggle with the angel brings to mind the Judaeo-Christian philosopher Marcel Ghelber. He is a Jew from eastern Europe, perhaps a new Shestov.[5] In the East, Jews often see arising in their midst thinkers who are attracted by Christianity but who remain on its fringes, adopting the role of debunkers of idols. In the West, on the other hand, faithful Jews in search of their identity ostensibly tend to ignore Christianity, seeking among Christians little more than political allies. It must be admitted that Romanian and Russian anti-Semitism has historically assumed bestial forms, such as to require from the churches of these countries a solemn act of repentance as well as the modification of certain liturgical texts. Nonetheless, from the perspective of a clinical "Marxian" analysis, one cannot overlook the sociological factors that contributed to this anti-Semitism. In western Ukraine, for example, Jews acted as intermediaries between the great Polish landowners and their Orthodox peasants. Deep down, the secret influence of Orthodoxy, filtering through this heavy historical burden, has nonetheless occasionally attracted certain Jews in the same way that Jewish mysticism has attracted certain Christians. Interestingly, the renaissance of two great spiritual traditions—Hesychasm in Orthodoxy, Hassidism in Judaism—occurred at the same time and in the same place: around 1800 in the region bordering on the Carpathian Mountains. Both traditions focused on a methodical invocation of the divine Name. Paisius Velichkovsky, who initiated the revival of Hesychasm, was a Ukrainian who had settled in Moldavia. He was the grandson of a Jewish woman from Poltava. Moreover, towards

---

[5] Lev Shestov was a Russian Jewish existentialist philosopher. He emigrated to France in 1921, fleeing from the aftermath of the October Revolution, and lived in Paris until his death in 1938. Though not well known today, he influenced many people, including Berdyaev, Bulgakov and Camus.

the end of the nineteenth century the Russian religious philosophers were themselves particularly attentive to Jewish thought. Soloviev, for example, studied Hebrew with a Rabbi. His teaching on Wisdom is full of insights from the Kabbalah, and he died praying for the Jewish people. In the twentieth century, Berdyaev not only fought against anti-Semitism but was inspired by Jewish prophetism. Even today, in Russia some of the boldest witnesses of Christianity are converted Jews who yet retain their humble, though indomitable, power as prophets.

Marcel Ghelber, who only recently came to live in the West, is "someone awestruck", to use his own phrase. In connection with Jacob's combat with the angel — with God — he writes: "Despite the best of pedagogical intentions, how naïve all apophatic theology appears, compared with the overwhelming implications of Jacob's struggle with God! Everything takes place as if in a hallucinatory state of seeming unreality, outside all ethics and all history. But, in fact, how fundamental is the Reality envisaged, disclosed — almost inconceivable and so terrible — by this struggle with God in an attempt to pin him down!"[6]

"Israel shall be thy name; for thou hast prevailed with God."[7]

---

[6] Ghelber came to the West from Romania in 1971, residing briefly in France before settling in French-speaking Switzerland. He died in 2000. The excerpt quoted can be found in *À la recherché de sa source et de son sens Divins: Vivre sa vie en Dieu et la vie de Dieu en soi.* (Lausanne: Éditions l'Age d'Homme, 2001), 56. This posthumous publication was selected by Claude Bridel from papers left by Ghelber, but Olivier Clément was familiar with the passage in question in the early 1970s, since he published some of Ghelber's writings in *Contacts*.

[7] Gen 32:28.

A people set apart, harshly purified by the Law and the disappointments of history, sifted to the point of becoming no more than a little remnant, a shoot, an expectation. Wandering ... A wound inflicted on history, when history becomes stable and settled. A people tempted by idolatry, and a wrecker of idols. Wounds inflicted but also wounds suffered. Existence is exile. And the Name is sanctified even in the hell of immanence, of pogroms, gas chambers and cremation ovens. An indestructible people, nourished and matured by the study of the Book, by the study of studies of the Book, by the rhythmic prayer of men who sway as they stand praying, in a language whose syllables are mellifluous and in which each letter is a number of the Emanation.[8] And the righteous man sets free in all things the sparks of an unrecognized Presence. For God too is in exile. I remember Martin Buber, when he was very old, saying that though it is a good thing to fast, even the act of eating with this liberating attentiveness might be tantamount to sanctity itself. And that the righteous pray not just with a passage from Scripture but with the wood of the floorboards on which they stand!

The God of the Bible is a "carnal" God who reserves the blood for himself and makes his mark on the male sex organ. The complaint of Job mingles with the love song of the Sulamite down the ages. The people await justice and long for the Promised Messianic Land; but the return there by force of arms and the driving of Ishmael into the desert have today raised the problem of justice not as a challenge but an ordeal. This is not the

---

[8] A reference to Kabbalistic concepts and to the Hebrew practice known as *gematria*, whereby each letter of the alphabet can be assigned a numerical rather than a phonetic value.

justice that one demands of God and of other people but that, crucially, one should demand of oneself. For the Messianic land should be a land of justice for all.

❖

The Spirit-guided evolutionary process that little by little was unfolding within me—a naked man faced with naked death—led me to the mystery of Jesus. Jesus, whom India "ex-carnates"[9] and makes into an avatar, a personal manifestation of the impersonal, with the result that the inner Christ becomes no more than the image of the Self. But what if the Self were the image of Christ?

Jesus, whom Judaism has wished to ignore, and has done so all the more thanks to a Christendom that become established and guilty of persecution, obscuring even the fact of his Jewishness. And so it was the entire Jewish people that became a "man of sorrows".

Jesus, whom Mohammed confesses as having been born of the Virgin and as being the seal of sanctity. Yet Islam denies that he was crucified, since for Mohammed the vivifying death of God was unthinkable. Today, however, violence, suffering, humiliation and the renewal movement have given rise, in the work of the greatest of the Arab poets, to an obsession with the crucified God who rises again—and with him the

---

[9] Clément makes clearer what he means by this neologism in another book: "For India there can be no such thing as in-carnation since flesh has no proper consistency. It is simply a mask, a game, and as it were the ephemeral condensation of the impersonal Absolute into which everything is reabsorbed. Its approach is not one of in-carnation but ex-carnation, for it is not a question of saving the world but of saving oneself from it, or rather of recognizing that it is illusory." See *Un respect têtu: Islam et Christianisme*, avec Mohamed Talbi (Paris: Nouvelle Cité, 1989), 151.

entire earth. Badr Shakir al-Sayyab, for example, who died in 1965, sang:[10]

> My heart is become earth, throbbing
> > with wheat, blossom
> > and sweet water
> My heart is water, an ear of corn
> Whose death is resurrection. It lives in him
> > who eats
> The dough, round as a little breast,
> > life's breast.

Jesus, whom I continued to catch a glimpse of in the Gospels. I had read them on and off since adolescence—reading, rejecting, trying to forget them, thinking that I had forgotten them, being unable not to go back to them. I was fascinated by his words, his presence, even his moments of silence. I was unable to finally make up my mind to relativize the importance of what he said, what he said about himself. To conveniently see him as just a privileged image of the inner man. As for making him the symbol or dynamic redeemer of a suffering proletariat, I had got rid of certain intellectual baggage, as I have already said, and wanted no more pretexts. However, still more was I unable to accept his outrageous pretensions to be more than human, to be human-divine; worse, to be more than divine, to be divine-human.

---

[10] Badr Shakir al Sayyab (1926–64) was an Iraqi poet, the eldest child of a date grower and shepherd. His experiments with free verse helped change the course of modern Arabic poetry. The publication in 1960 of his third volume, *Song of Rain*, was one of the most significant events in contemporary Arabic poetry and has been compared to Eliot's *The Waste Land*. The above quotation is from "Christ after the Crucifixion", as translated by Ben M. Bennani.

I had gone into debt to acquire an icon of Christ from an antique dealer on the Boulevard Saint-Germain. More precisely, it was a triptych in *repoussé* and enamelled copper. I still have it on my desk. In the middle is Christ in the act of blessing: "Come, ye blessed of my Father".[11] On either side stand the Mother and the Friend, Mary and John the Forerunner. In Greek this type of composition is called a *deisis*, from a word meaning intercession or supplication. Mary and John are interceding or, rather, bearing witness to the fact that this Judge, by virtue of the cross—which, as Maximus the Confessor says, is a "judgment of judgment"—is in reality also our friend and bridegroom. At the time, I didn't know any of these beautiful things, though I would learn about them little by little. I interpreted things in my own way, and this time it is accredited "Orthodox" who will smile. On either side of that enigmatic Face, Woman and Man represented for me not just the Old and New Testaments (that much I did know) but, on the one hand, the cosmic femininity of Indian and other ancient religions, purified and rendered malleable by the Spirit; and, on the other hand, the worn-out faces of the prophets in the wilderness, proclaiming transcendence at the very moment when transcendence transcends itself to become this enigmatic Face. I was especially intrigued by the halo with a cross inside and the Greek inscription *ho ōn*: "he who is". Here, being is depicted not as the antechamber of some undifferentiated abyss, nor yet as a perfect individual who is enclosed in heaven, but as the "inside" of a "him", a personal presence who enters into communion. This face was like an enigma, with its claim to be an *I am* that would constitute the source of being.

---

[11] Mt 25:34.

The face of Buddha is heavy with eternity and closed in on itself, the eyes shut as if he is dissolved in his own rotundity. The typical Western portrait is open but ambiguously so, often having something ephemeral and sorrowful about it. It speaks of difference, sometimes of similarity, but nothing more. The face of Jesus, on the other hand, is light with eternity, and always open. It speaks of difference, but also of sameness.

There before me was this face with the unconditional welcome of those eyes that, after being closed on the cross and opened again on Easter morning, no longer terrify. At the time, all around me so many faces were becoming closed books; or, rather, it was I myself who was closing them. My head was spinning. Yet this face was there in the background, offering an unconditional welcome—"In him there is only Yes"[12]—whilst I for my part descended into my own little underworld.

Jesus—I encountered him, loved him, challenged him, let myself be challenged by him both in my relations with my fellow men and with the gods of other religions.

I was suffering from the dizziness of a freedom that was empty. I had burned my bridges. Being someone of no real culture, having no faith, and obeying no laws that had matured within a community sure of where it was going, what I loved about Jesus was what I called the "profaner" in him. I was wrong, because it was not the profane that he instituted. Let us leave that to the defunct theologians of the defunct "death of God" theology. What then did he institute? Perhaps simply that things should be what they are, but seen in a certain light. Perhaps just the fact that death no longer weighs heavy on one's heart and that faces open up. Perhaps simply that everything should be renewed. I

---

[12] Cf. 2 Cor 1:20.

was wrong and I right: he didn't institute profanity, but he did demolish all that "supernatural" science of the pure and the impure, the whole hierarchy of disdain and exclusions that weighed down the society of his day and that we too ceaselessly proliferate in order to protect ourselves from death. As for him, he settled his score with death in quite a different way. For he was free. That's it, that's exactly what I trying to say: it was freedom that he instituted, the creative sovereignty of love. And that he demonstrated even when in hellish agony, as when he says to the thief who is dying by his side—but who retains the ultimate freedom to choose between aversion and conversion—"Today you will be with me in paradise".[13]

And as for the recipes of the master chefs of the sacral, he well and truly set the cat among the pigeons. What a shot in the arm for those they had written off, big or small! This young rabbi takes his meals with anyone, and that at a time when a communal meal constituted a veritable rite, accompanied by meticulous rules of purification and selection. How modern he sounds when, referring to the consumption of food, he reminds his listeners of the most prosaic of biological functions, pointing out that what counts comes from the heart, that is to say from the most personal part of a person. He goes to that "lost centre", and those who have a broken and wounded heart go to him. In doing so he wallows in ritual impurity, disgraces himself, associates with women, heretics, pagans and tax collectors who are in cahoots with the occupier. To the old notions of pure and impure that the Pharisees harden themselves with, he prefers the monetary imagery that would easily be understood in these marginalized

---

[13] Luke 23:43.

circles. Images whose religious neutrality is precisely what facilitates the opening up of the person. Jesus is certainly a profaner par excellence—and with what violence!—when he lays into the Pharisees, though apparently they were very good people who scrupulously fulfilled their duties to their fellowmen and to God. But to the prostitute who throws herself at Jesus' feet much will be forgiven because she loved much. I believe, help thou my unbelief! I love you, help my lack of love! I am crucified—whether on your right hand or your left I don't know. I am full of blasphemy, and faith.

Profaner! To all those sure of themselves, whether in the Church or in a party, he proclaims—and with what irony!—that the Sabbath is made for man not man for the Sabbath, and that he did not come for those who are well but for the sick. But who *is* well? Who is sick? Those evangelical reversals ... Blessed are the poor in spirit. Publicans and prostitutes are entering the Kingdom before you. Let him who has no sin cast the first stone.

An elusive, unclassifiable profaner who drove the money changers out of the Temple with a whip but who—and with what dignity!—makes Peter put away his sword. Who re-establishes the original, paradisal plenitude of human love, and frees man from family nests of vipers.[14] Let the dead bury the dead. Whoever loves his father or mother or son or daughter more than me is not worthy of me. He is sovereignly free, in fact, and above all from the passions of *eros* and power. Puritans, would you allow a courtesan to pour perfume over your feet and let her wipe them with

---

[14] Probably an allusion to *Le Nœud de vipères*, the 1932 novel by the Catholic writer François Mauriac, which deals with family intrigue.

her hair? Libertines, would you allude at that point to your tomb?[15] And that requirement of love for one's enemies, that example given even when on the cross: "Father, forgive them for they know not what they do". It is the only possible way—in history too—of breaking ineluctable chains of events: he who takes up the sword perishes by the sword. How liberated, as light as light itself, is he who can offer the other cheek! In fact, he walks on water. Jesus goes straight to each person, prefers each one, thereby profaning all impersonal sacrality, whether it goes by the name of religion, history, structure or system. For the only thing in which you should rejoice is that your "names" are written in heaven. Jesus sees the face behind the mask, breaks the heart of stone to free a heart of flesh; discerns and releases in each person that part which is divine, the image of eternity. He talks not of what is forbidden and what is allowed, but calls for creative love. He breathes the Spirit. He goes straight to the collaborator and the resistance fighter, to the marginalized and the capitalist. He doesn't theorize, or perform miracles to change stones into bread, yet the bread is his body and the wine his blood. Whoever eats this body and drinks this blood has eternal life, already here below. Son of a king, he refuses to be made king. He simply cross-references the reign of Caesar to that of God, and introduces into history—like a wound, like leaven—the revelation of personhood and the all-humanity of each person. Ever since, this has been the secret axis of history. An axis of fire—"I have come to cast fire upon the earth"—from which proceeds everything creative of truth, life or beauty.

---

[15] This conflation of Luke with Matthew and John is precisely what is found in the Orthodox hymns for Holy Week.

One often finds in the Gospels a sort of irony that attracts like a magnet, that awakens, that allows glimpses of a God who is strangely unknown. The Samaritan woman talks about water as being a burden, but Jesus speaks of water that is living. The Canaanite woman mentions the crumbs the dogs gather from under the table, when faced with Jewish exclusivism, but it is the universality of his message that Jesus unleashes. It is the irony of a King and of an Innocent. I was surprised that Christians didn't take more notice of the charismatic side of Jesus, his noble, regal, radiant way of being present and yet of stepping aside, of provoking and letting the blows pass through him as if into the void, of turning questions around, of speaking like an archer shoots and of keeping silent, of escaping to go and pray in solitude during the night, "separated from all and united to all".[16] The way that on the cross are placed royalty and innocence, the Word and silence, presence and withdrawal, history and the Kingdom. Perhaps the Christ of the Dormition at Sopoćani in Serbia—the Serbs are a warrior people—best expresses this paradoxical royalty, this dazzling virility that is yet full of tenderness. One of our most recent poets, Yves Bonnefoy, remarked on this in an admirable passage—one which incited me to actually visit Sopoćani.[17]

---

[16] The definition of a monk given by Evagrius of Pontus (d. 399). See *On Prayer*, §124, in *The Philokalia*, vol. 4, 69.

[17] The famous thirteenth-century fresco of the Dormition of the Mother of God is discussed in Yves Bonnefoy, *The Lure and Truth of Painting: Selected Essays on Art*, ed. Richard Stamelman (Chicago & London: University of Chicago Press, 1995), 21–2. The chapter in question—"Byzance"—was first published as an article in 1961.

What struck me about the Gospels, in contrast to what we tend to find in myths, was their modernity and historical nature. What little knowledge I had of Hassidic tales—those first-hand accounts of paradoxical rabbis of the eighteenth and nineteenth centuries—helped me to be aware of this historicity. To be more precise, the historicity of the miracles—despite the fudging and the many reservations of the exegetes.

Jacques Masui is one of the people to whom francophone countries owe the most for the discovery in our time of the spiritual traditions of the world. He encouraged the translation and assured the publication of the most valuable of texts, notably the *Petite Philocalie de la prière du cœur*. One day he said to me that, for anyone who has been awakened to Jewish spirituality by such Hassidic tales, an episode in the Gospels such as the one of the woman with a flow of blood rings strikingly true, something impossible to invent. The people who appear in the Gospels have a personal depth—sometimes incongruous, sometime tragic—that is not found in myths. We move from myth to reality. Faces win out over symbols, newness over repetition.

However, myth is not entirely abolished, and here is precisely the difference from the Old Testament. With the Gospels, we have the advent of persons. That is to say, as in the Bible as a whole, encounter and faith. But also, above and beyond linear time—by virtue of the waves that have been rippling outwards ever since the implosion of eternity into time—there is also an embracing of the primordial. Participation in myth is not rejected, as it was in the Old Testament; it is taken up again, becoming the interiority of communion, the flesh of the Spirit. Which is why those theologians who retain the faith but reject religion turn this prodigious marriage of God with the earth into a rather sad *mariage blanc,* a marriage in name only, unconsummated.

Take, for instance, the conversation with Nicodemus. When Jesus tells him that one must be "born again", this wise man of Israel says mockingly, "How can a man [...] enter a second time into his mother's womb?"[18] Here speaks the wisdom of Israel indeed. The curt biblical revelation of a unique and short-lived individual existence, and of a history that is linear, aimed towards an end, as opposed to the nostalgia for renewal characteristic of ancient religions with their cyclic conception of time. In a ritual orgy, man regresses to the state of a seed in the womb of Mother Earth, in the hope of renewing himself. In ancient China certain techniques for longevity involved adopting a fetal position, living in a closed circuit as it were, and slowing down one's breathing to an extreme point. Even today, our society is haunted by incest. The taboo against incest forces us the hard way to face up to the reality of the other, of history, of death. We would like to return to the mother's womb, if not to be reborn then at least to forget. I am not sure that certain forms of ecological pontificating, which are often accompanied by a Hinduistic sensitivity, are not connected with this same nostalgia. So there you have the wisdom of Nicodemus (and of Sigmund Freud, that other teacher of Israel despite his foolish sayings regarding Moses): the mother is lost for ever; we must die.

So Jesus repeats his affirmation, but this time with an important precision: we must be reborn of water and the Spirit.

Thus the age-old symbol of water—as tomb and womb—becomes, in the Spirit, the vital requirement

[18] Jn 3:4.

for a personal encounter with Jesus. There is a Pentecost at the heart of the myth, in the midst of the earth, which connects—though in terms of a Face—with the cosmic Pentecost of the origins, when the Spirit breathed upon the waters. When the wind caused primordial matter to stir, as it still does today the sand on the beaches—or in a Zen garden. The humanity of Jesus seems not to be separated from anything, from anyone. Not by way of fusion; the distinctions of Genesis persist in the Gospels, but everything is gathered together without confusion in a person. Jesus is separated from nothing, because he welcomes and awakens, because he uses the universe eucharistically. Because his humanity is not closed in on itself by death, yet without being consumed either—unlike those Hindu sages described as "liberated whilst still alive" that the texts liken to sheets of paper that have just been burnt and on which the writing is still legible. That is, so long as no breath of wind disperses everything into ashes! A relationship between man and God is revealed that is neither separation nor fusion, but a sharing of a love that allows for the irradiation of the divine and the transfiguration of the human. Yes, God reveals himself as different and the more unknown the more he is known. An abyss, to be sure, and entirely other. But from the abyss comes a freely offered love for an exchange of lives. An abyss of difference within sameness: "In the beginning was the Word, and the Word was (reaching out) towards God, and the Word was God."[19] Sameness, but within

---

[19] Jn 1:1. Clément inserts in brackets the word *tendu* (here translated as "reaching out") to underline the implication in the normal meaning (i.e. "towards" rather than "with") of the preposition πρὸς, which is used in the Greek original and

tension. Hence the paradoxical possibility for this God-other-than-God to go out of his transcendence without doing away with it or without at the same time causing the universe to vanish into thin air: "I came forth from the Father and have come into the world".[20] The paradoxical possibility of descending into his own absence, of "emptying" himself, of "humbling" himself, as Paul says. Of becoming Job, even though from now on the hand that closed Job's mouth is pierced. Of taking man's side on the cross, in the hell of dereliction, God separated from God. The side of naked man buried in naked anguish. My God, my God, why have you forsaken me? Adam, where are you? My God, where are you? Night in broad daylight. Night in the heart of God. But then: "the Father and I are one".[21] Christ is risen and everything is risen with him. Despite the many dead, all the anguish, all the absurdities, all the horrors and all the despair, clots of blood fall from the face of God and the Man of Sorrows rises. And everything rises with him. He is in everything. Everything is in him. Rachel's children are resurrected, and Lazarus leaps from the tomb, this time definitively. The smell of roast fish by the lakeside, the hair—oh so long!—of the courtesan, the time when he makes them sit down on the grass to share the five loaves, and that other when Peter was forgiven, and each second of your own miserable life—all of it is resurrected! Everything begins anew, and one can try to love since death is no more, since death itself is filled with God.

    which conveys the idea of reciprocal communion between the Son and the Father.

[20] Jn 16:28.
[21] Jn 10:30.

But where is all that, where?
In the wind that gets up.
Jesus is risen and the wind gets up. From now on it "blows where it wishes, and you hear the sound of it, but cannot tell where it comes from and where it goes. So is everyone who is born of the Spirit".[22]

The Spirit was no longer anonymous. From now on it had the face of Jesus, face of faces. The Spirit has many other faces. Man born of the Spirit is no longer simply this flesh that is rotting already, of which one knows only too well where it comes from and where it is going. The Spirit permeates even the flesh of his body, which is assimilated to the glorious body of the Risen One. "He who believes in me [...] out of his heart will flow rivers of living water", since in Jesus "dwells all the fullness of the Godhead *bodily*".[23] Man born of the Spirit no longer has a beginning or an end, since in Christ he comes from the Father and returns to him. Liberated while still alive, indeed! Not a spherical sage, however, but a murderer or a prostitute who has had a change of heart. Like the wind that carries them and fills them, they are recognized by a sound. The wind makes the forest and the sea sing. When Elijah went to the mountain for his appointment with God, God was not in the roar of the storm and tempest but in a "still small voice", bordering on silence. In the man born of the Spirit, God hums a tune and the world becomes music. The Spirit rests upon Jesus, causing him to rejoice. Silence is at the heart of the Word. The Spirit is the unction of the Son and the Kingdom of the

---

[22] Jn 3:8.
[23] Jn 7:38; Col 2:9.

Father. The Spirit reveals the hidden face of the earth. The Spirit is the Land of the Living.[24]

✣

In a way my exploration of the various spiritual traditions of the world made easier my approach to the Gospels. For I already knew instinctively that reality could not be contained within that clear-cut, quantifiable segment that our reason and our senses are able to dissect and objectify. I knew that another kind of knowledge existed, one inseparable from asceticism, and that if man integrates himself and at the same time empties himself, he becomes the admirable instrument—almost in the sense of a musical instrument—of this knowledge of God. I had furtively glimpsed those patches of light and peace in which things glow and when faces light up. Which is why the miracles recounted in the Gospels did not bother me. Everything is full of miracles, and I suppose that for the most part they are related to precise laws concerning those "different", more obscure, more opaque—or, rather, more transparent—states of what we call "matter". Children,

---

[24] This phrase—a favourite one, as mentioned in our Introduction—is here unusually but not inappropriately applied to the Holy Spirit. The phrase, as seen, comes from the inscription on the mosaic of Christ Pantocrator in the Church of the Holy Saviour in Chora, Constantinople. Given Clément's interest in countering the writings of such thinkers as Nietzsche, it is interesting to note how he refers to the fresco of the Resurrection (the Harrowing of Hell) in this same church when discussing Nietzsche's comment that he "could only believe in a God who dances". "But", writes Clément, "Christ *is* this 'God who dances'! ... In this picture Christ descends into hell, breaking the doors of hell with one foot; and with the other foot he begins a process of re-ascension in a shining whiteness, and he pulls up Adam and Eve from their tombs. There he is, the 'God who dances'!" See *Taizé: A Meaning to Life*, 26.

"innocent" people and poets know a little about that. We all know it, once we have left behind, I do not say the West (which is anyway everywhere nowadays), but the writings of the exegetes. In my village, the secular, socialist rationality reigned supreme. Yet everyone found it normal that two or three ordinary individuals—typically they live at the end of the street or in a somewhat distant farmhouse—should be able to cure the most "physical" of ailments by means of nothing other than their "spirit". It is taken for granted and never commented upon. Just like Chinese Marxists with their traditional medicine. Not to mention, of course, the simple fact of existing at all, and of continuing to exist. We must radicalize the words of Bernanos that "all is grace"[25] and say, with no third choice, either that all is nothingness or else all is a miracle!

What struck me about the Gospel miracles was that there were so few of them and that they were always significant. "Signs", John calls them. For his parables, Jesus chooses the language and imagery of sensible things; but it is from among the teeming possibilities of the invisible that he chooses "signs" of the great transformation, the great explosion of life that he came to realize. Jesus is transparent, I said to myself, to those expanses of light and peace of which we merely catch fleeting glimpses, since in the depths of his being there is no death, just the Breath. Why should it be surprising, then, that peace and light should shine from him, transforming men and things? However, it is the irradi-

---

[25] These are the last words of the main character, a young priest dying of cancer, in the 1936 novel by George Bernanos, *The Diary of a Country Priest*. But Bernanos is simply repeating verbatim what St Thérèse of Lisieux had said (in June 1897) towards the very end of her life, as she lay slowly and painfully dying from tuberculosis.

ance of a person, and only a personal faith can receive it: "Your faith has made you whole".

Moreover, when he performed miracles, Jesus refused to replace communion with compulsion. He did not change the stones to bread (though he is often criticized for this today!). He did not come down from the cross or show himself, resuscitated and resplendent, to the Jewish and Roman authorities. And so the real miracle was born: that of our freedom.

Similarly, Christ's resurrection seemed to me to be nothing other than the truth about life, a life so powerful that it conquers death in all its aspects. Only, everything is to be turned upside down, beginning with the way we look at the world. We have become so accustomed to being surrounded by death that the full manifestation of life seems to us unbelievable.

No, what bothered me—I must get round to it or, rather, come back to it—was the exclusiveness of Jesus. For I had no wish to falsify what he says about himself, as do those Gnostics big and little who take themselves, individually or all together, for the Christ—not *in* him, but *instead of* him. What bothered me was Jesus' claim to be the sole mediator. Not one of those who show the way, who reveal the truth and the life, but to be himself the very Way, the Truth and the Life. There was also that unclassifiable sudden appearance of the divine Unknown that I mentioned earlier. And then, too, this unity with the Father that he maintained was his. His *Father!* Not some supreme identity with the Self, but a unity within difference, personal and privileged. Moreover, one in which he includes us, simply because he wishes to, by a free act of love. "My Father and yours," he says. "That they may be one as we are one." As for the transcendent oneness of all religions, a common esotericism, a *philosophia perennis* à la Huxley, not to speak of a certain Christian "dialectic" of the sort that says, "Each to his truth, let's discuss things". Well, no! That wouldn't do! Either Jesus—and he alone—embodied the transcendent oneness of all religions and Christianity was "the religion of religions"—and, I would say, of everything else—or else he was insane and I might as well have done with him.

✛ 5 ✛

Berdyaev

THE FIRST PERSON to make me understand that it was possible to be a Christian, the first in my case to tip the scales in favour of the Gospel and away from India, was Nicolas Berdyaev. I never met him personally. He died in 1948, the same year that I arrived in Paris. Strangely, though, his last article and my first (which was entirely historical in nature) both appeared in the same review, *Cheval Blanc*. This was edited by a patient teacher, an expert in the Socratic art of maieutics, who gathered round himself an oddly colourful team of seekers of the Absolute who were also involved in experimental community-based living.[1] Berdyaev liked young people who were in search of creative spirituality. On the eve of his death, at the height of his fame—published in translation all over the world from the United States to Japan, recently made a doctor honoris causa by the University of Cambridge, and considered by many (especially in the English-speaking world) to be a prophet of the new times—he had had no hesitation in collaborating with this review, obscure as it was, since its approach to things seemed to him to be fertile.

---

[1] Among their number was Lanza del Vasto, a disciple of Gandhi, who had just founded the Community of the Ark, intended to be a model alternative non-violent society.

What a destiny this man had! With a mother who was half-French and a wife who was Catholic, here was a Russian destined for every kind of encounter: whether between Russia and Europe, between the Christian West and the Christian East, or between atheism and the Gospel. He was relentless in his efforts to find a new language with which to express the newness of the Spirit, and persistent in seeking to incorporate the challenge of Marx and Nietzsche into a divine-humanity.[2]

A handsome, veritable Rosenkavalier in his youth, he had experienced all the temptations of a Stavrogin[3]—that is, had sought to make himself loved only in order to destroy. Certain fools say, smugly, that he suffered from a nervous tic that caused him to stick his tongue out involuntarily from time to time. (I hope he stuck it out at them! Just as he had done to Dzerzhinsky, the man who established and headed the Soviet secret police.[4]) At the end of the nineteenth century, this young nobleman broke with his own social background, began to frequent workers and Jews, and became one of the pioneers of Marxism in Russia. All the same, he believed that personal consciousness and its values could not simply be attributed to a deterministic historical process. Thus he wished to combine

---

[2] Clément clarifies elsewhere how he understands this term: "Christian revelation is a revelation of human nature not just of the divine" (*Mémoires*, 103).
[3] The central character in Dostoevsky's novel, *Demons*.
[4] A reference to the fact that when Dzerzhinsky came in person to interrogate him, Berdyaev gave him a dressing-down on the problems with Bolshevism and the way the revolution had turned into totalitarianism, disregarding the freedom of the individual. Not only was he not put on trial but was set free. On this episode, see later in this chapter.

the thought of Marx with that of Kant. For he was of the opinion not simply that there could be no genuine revolution without freedom of spirit but that only the spirit was truly revolutionary![5]

The first time he was imprisoned by the imperial regime he had had an intense experience of human communion. Later he was banished for some three years to the north of the country, for he had now become one of the leaders and thinkers of Russian Marxist socialism. This was at a time when, all over Europe, Marxism was still open-minded and finding its way. But when the Bolshevik Party was formed, he detected in it almost immediately "the spirit of the Grand Inquisitor". His discovery (especially through Nietzsche) of tragedy and creativity, his encounter with the Gospel (via Dostoevsky and, shortly afterwards, the Greek Fathers)—all of this, including his mysterious experience of blood and chaos during the revolution of 1905, led him to switch from materialism to "spiritual realism". At Petersburg, with a purity as of fire, he endured the immanentist and Dionysiac temptations of the so-called "new religious conscience", with its anarchic and erotic mysticism. To all this he opposed Christ, as revelation of what it means to be a person and of true freedom. After becoming Orthodox (though remaining on the periphery of the Church), he sought to develop a creative spirituality that might help exorcize the chaos. A spirituality that would apply not just to individuals but that would be able to shed light on history in general. (One might compare his

---

[5] The thinking behind these words is not only reflected in the title of Berdyaev's book *Spirit and Freedom*, but surely also inspired the title of Clément's own 1979 book, *La Révolte de l'Esprit*. In fact, its epigraph is taken from Berdyaev's spiritual autobiography.

efforts to Gandhi's attempt to bring India's spirituality into the realm of history.) He called upon the revolutionary intelligentsia to reject all attempts to turn politics into a "religion", proposing instead a renewed Christianity that would be capable both of relativizing politics and inspiring a form of action that would be patient yet creative. In one of his books, published in 1910, he endeavours to distinguish between socialism as a form of religion and the human truth of socialism. By which he meant managing social and economic life in a way that would facilitate, so far as is possible, the influence of the spiritual in human relationships and in the workplace.

During the First World War, Berdyaev envisaged the foundations of a Europe in which the Russian genius and the French genius would complement each other. He denounced the instability, the weakness and the false femininity of the Russian soul, doomed as it was, he maintained—unless it generated an authentic spiritual virility from its own resources—to being raped by its German or Bolshevik counterparts. The empty words spouted by the February revolutionaries disgusted him. Amid the chaos that he had long felt coming, he nevertheless faced up to his responsibilities, intervening between the troops and the demonstrators. He was elected to the "democratic congress", which was a sort of pre-parliament. October, with the violence which followed and which quickly became systematic, led him to wonder what "demons", in Dostoevsky's sense, were masterminding the Russian Revolution. In an article written in 1918 for the journal *De Profundis*, he foresaw the whole of Stalinism. Nonetheless, he decided to stay in Russia, for he accepted the revolution as a chastisement resulting from the nature of the former society, as well as being the consequence of a

Christianity become incapable of inspiring a culture or of proclaiming and realizing the social dimension of the Gospel. Beneath all the bloody toiling of bodies and souls he sensed in many people an openness to the fundamental things. Then he came across a veritable *starets*, Father Alexis Metchev.[6] Even though he was a simple married priest, Father Alexis had the gift of discernment—concerning historical events, too. For him, the salvation of the Russian people could only come from its own spiritual renewal. Any foreign intervention would be harmful.

Berdyaev was arrested again, twice, but Dzerzhinsky had him released after the philosopher had explained his position with total frankness: a position of political loyalty combined with spiritual freedom, with a vocation to sow seeds of spirituality in the new society that was taking shape. Berdyaev also had some support, albeit precarious, from Lunacharsky, the People's Commissar for Education. Lunacharsky was the only Bolshevik leader genuinely interested, at the dawn of the new century, in a renewal of Russian and European culture.[7] And then we find Berdyaev, at his own risk, involved in a fruitful venture: proclaiming to audiences of workers that only the Spirit is revolutionary ("Spirit" with a capital letter now); lecturing at Moscow University; and founding the *Free Academy of Spiritual Culture*, which functioned in the evening in premises that were

---

[6] Now canonized.

[7] Active as an art critic and journalist throughout his political career, he was also a prolific writer, penning essays on Pushkin and Proust, among others. He corresponded with H. G. Wells and George Bernard Shaw and was associated with the foundation of the Bolshoi Drama Theatre. He also argued in favour of the preservation of historic buildings, which certain elements in the Bolshevik Party wished to destroy.

initially loaned to him but which were later forbidden. He became vice-president of the Union of Writers, and lectured on the spirituality of Dostoevsky—for he hailed him as a great spiritual thinker not just a great psychologist—at precisely the moment when Lenin was consigning him to the dustbins of the revolution. He extracted from history its divine-human meaning even as, little by little, materialism was becoming the official philosophy of an "a-theocracy".

In 1922, that fateful year, Lenin did make some concessions in economic and social life, but at the same time he reinforced the ideological dictatorship of the party. Berdyaev was exiled, not for any political reason, but for spiritual opposition. And so we find our philosopher in Berlin, where the chaos was no less present but where, at least on the surface, things seem to be organized. It was there that he published *A New Middle Ages* (also translated as *The End of Our Time*), which gained him a worldwide reputation. He was in no way advocating a return to the Middle Ages, but maintained that it was the Middle Ages alone that had been able to accumulate the spiritual energy on which modern humanism subsisted. Now that humanism had used up these reserves, it was turning into anti-humanism, the death of God bringing in its wake the death of man. There remained only two options: either a disintegration into nothingness or else the discovery of man as made in the image of God, as "microcosm and micro-theos". The future, he argued, belongs to a divine-humanity in which there would be a place for the sort of exploration of what it means to be human such as the major modern atheists have conducted, with their demands for justice and creativity.

Berdyaev next settled in Paris, in the suburb of Clamart. He kept open house *à la russe* with the result that his residence became a great meeting-place between East and West, for he had no wish to be a simple emigrant. Working to keep alive Russian religious thought—which had now been silenced in the USSR—he took part in the foundation of the journal *Esprit*, which mainly aimed to promote the philosophical approach known as Personalism.[8] He attended the Décades de Pontigny, where the intelligentsia gathered.[9] He also brought about ecumenical meetings—the first, it seems, ever to be held in Paris—in which he introduced some participants to the Greek Fathers, and others to the social dimension of neighbourly love, always maintaining a balance between the historical process and the Spirit.

After the war broke out, he encouraged spiritual resistance—especially in favour of the Jews—among the Russian Orthodox circles in France, which were at the time tragically divided. The occupying forces struck his entourage but he himself was saved at death's door by a senior German officer in the mould of an Ernst Jünger, who admired his work. In the aftermath of the conflict, he believed in the possibility of the lasting transformation of the Soviet regime, and so promoted returns to Russia. He wrote *The Russian Idea* in order to help the youth over there rediscover and build on the history of their country. He himself was prepared to return, but only on condition that his works be published in his homeland. They were not,

---

[8] Berdyaev contributed an article entitled "Vérité et mensonge du Communisme" to the very first issue (October 1932).

[9] The Décades de Pontigny were gatherings of intellectuals, held almost every year from 1910 to 1939, in the former Cistercian Abbey of Pontigny in Burgundy. For ten days (hence the term "decade") discussions were held on literary, philosophical or religious subjects.

given the hardening of Stalin's position after the war. So history inflicted upon him the trial of a Job, and he never did return. Yet he never lost his faith in what alone was essential: freedom and the Spirit. Before his death—which came suddenly and while he was still hard at work—Berdyaev requested that in his house (which he had bequeathed to the Church) a chapel should be installed and dedicated to the Holy Spirit.

During the war, I had found in the library of a friend's house in Aquitaine a book by him that was translated as *Freedom and the Spirit*. I had read it at one go, spending a whole day and night in the process. Much of what it said escaped me, but it did seem to discuss the most important thing. I mean a Christianity capable of meeting the needs of contemporary man and his nakedness in the face of death, love and beauty. Capable, what's more, of taking stock of the evolutionary development of world religions which I was then investigating. Admittedly, as I was later to realize, Berdyaev at times goes to extremes or is one-sided. He creates myths and gets caught in his own game, as with the poetics of uncreated freedom that he devised, based on the vocabulary of Jacob Boehme. At the time I was quite incapable of such discrimination. Yet a different way of thinking, a different sensibility had branded me for ever. And the branding iron was in the form of a cross. A cross and a rose, for "it is by the mystery of the cross that the rose of universal existence will flower again".[10]

---

[10] This esoteric Judaeo-Christian quotation is presumably from a Rosicrucian publication. In Alchemy and Rosicrucianism, the rose at the centre of the cross symbolizes regeneration, the individual's unfolding consciousness. We should remember that at this stage Clément was still searching for truth among the various religions of the world. In *Le Visage intérieur*

Turns of phrase à la Berdyaev crop up all by themselves in my writings. For example, that the time is past for thinking in terms of God versus man or man versus God. What truly counts is divine-humanity, for which everything has been created. Religions stress certain aspects of it, atheism others. It is a Christ-like divine-humanity that we are called to propagate in freedom and the Spirit. God awaits man's creative response. In Christ, God reveals himself to man; in the Spirit, man should reveal himself to God. There thus ensues a prodigious exchange of lives: the face of God in man, the face of man in God. And then there are Berdyaev's invectives against those who have made God a monster or a stony-hearted Being. No, God is sacrificial love. He bears within himself his eternal other and, lo and behold, the face of this other is reflected in that of man. God longs for his other, for man. In creating man he made himself vulnerable to the point of being crucified. His all-powerfulness is thus as weak as love but, like love, tenacious and radiant. By his absence, by his own withdrawal—Boehme's *Ungrund*, said Berdyaev (though it is not true)—God allows man's sombre freedom, his terrible and proud freedom, to spring forth. And man, this "Adam Kadmon"[11] that we all are, ravages the relative in his thirst

> (published not long after the present book, in 1978) Clément reminds us that this same image is to be found in the Armenian and Syriac traditions: "The rose blooms on the cross. In the cruciferous halo of the Transfigured One, his face, says the Armenian Church—heir to the ancient Syrian tradition—is the 'resplendent Rose'" (p. 44).

[11] This is the Kabbalah's term for the primordial man, though it is in Berdyaev that Clément would have encountered it. In Berdyaev's *Dialectique existentielle du divin et de l'humain* (1947), for example, we find the following: "It may be said that a pre-eternal manhood exists in God. The pre-eternal

for the absolute. He wrests creation from its Creator, objectifying it into opaqueness and absence. Thus evil and the struggle against evil constitute the very proof of the existence of God, the Innocent One, whose face trickles with blood in the shadows. Hence the cross, hence the paradox of a God who by his humiliation disarms our fierce, frozen freedom. One divine-human drop of blood is enough to transform the world secretly. Our task is to discern, reveal and manifest this transformation so that the God-man might become God-humanity and God-universe. For the Church is nothing other than the world in the process of deification. Not a single blade of grass grows that is not in the Church, not a single galaxy exists that does not celebrate in the Church the cosmic liturgy. There is no creative deed that does not manifest the Church nor cause to shine forth in this world of death the light of the Eighth Day. Any profoundly religious act is creative. The desert ascetic recreates himself in the divine light, assimilating the dark face of the earth into his own transfigured face. Conversely, any truly creative act is religious. This is true not simply of someone who creates beauty, but of anyone who fights for justice and dignity, of a mother when she arouses a smile on the face of her child, or of lovers who are experiencing the true certainty of their love. All in their own way shatter the mask of death, revealing and fashioning in light the face of Christ, he who is to come. Admittedly, creativity has its tragic side. History, too. A creative artist would like to transfigure the world, but can only

---

Man exists, whom the Kabbalah calls [Adam Kadmon]." R.M. French's translation—*The Divine and the Human* (London: G. Bles, 1959, 111–12)—alters Berdyaev's original to read "the heavenly Adam".

create signs. True creativity is marked by the sign of the cross. Yet the fulfilment of things is under way, and even our failures mysteriously add fuel to a fire whose sparks are multiplying. The coming of the Kingdom is actively awaited. When Marx speaks out against the obsession with consumer goods or the social objectifying of man, he is in the Church. Just as Nietzsche is when—in opposition to the hedonism of "the last man"[12]—he calls for a creative surpassing of ourselves. For God became man so that man might become god.

And so I turned to the Christians.

---

[12] "The last man" is a term used by Nietzsche in *Thus Spoke Zarathustra* to describe the antithesis of the imagined superior being, the Übermensch. "The last man" takes no risks, lacks individuality and creativity, and seeks only comfort and security.

✢ 6 ✢

Sicut Cervus

First of all, I had to overcome a certain repugnance that had taken root in my childhood and become instinctive.[1] Catholicism had been presented to me—oh, by discreet allusions, but I knew how to read the signs—as a vast, crafty, repressive and "castrating" earthly power structure. Witness the Inquisition, the female prisoners in that tower with its enigmatic *régister*, and those celibate men in their dresses. As for Protestantism, I had been taught that it merely represented a stage on the road to secularism and socialism—a stage that was now past.

On the other hand, the actual Catholics and Protestants that I met—and I came across many in the Resistance—did not disappoint me. They knew, for example, how to set limits to the violence they occasionally had to practise—an honourable limit, such as Albert Camus writes about.[2] Others, who had been tempted by the

---

[1] For the title of this chapter, "Sicut cervus", the first words of Psalm 42 have been used: "As the hart [panteth after the water brooks, so panteth my soul after thee, O God]." It was to this psalm that Clément was alluding when he wrote in Chapter 1 (see page 8) of how his ancestors sang Marot's setting of verses describing the "thirsting of the spiritual deer".

[2] An allusion to a stance taken by Camus in his *Lettre à un ami allemand* (published in 1948 but partially written during the Occupation) and in *L'Homme révolté* (1951).

Vichy regime during the first two or three years of the war, were now disillusioned and like all who feel that history is running away from them made do with a sudden onset of apocalypticism. At the time, Christian circles, Christian families, proved to be one of the country's strengths. Nevertheless, there was no doubt that a certain kind of legalistic moralism prevailed over the paradoxes of the Gospel. With regard to sexuality in particular, this could easily turn into a back-to-front understanding of the sacred, an unholy fascination with the impure.

I noticed fairly soon that, despite their high moral standards, people from these stable Christian circles would nonetheless all too easily react with fear or disdain when confronted with those on the fringes of life or society. An entire strand of the Gospel message—which teaches that Christianity is a matter not of law but of creative love, not a question of pure versus impure but of persons and freedom—well, they knew about this of course, but didn't often put it into practice in their daily lives. Except in a few cases, the parable of the workers who came at the eleventh hour didn't go down at all well. But, I would add today, was it ever otherwise? And who has the right to judge? The prodigal son has no right to judge his elder brother. All in all, though, in the Christian circles that I came across I did meet many people of genuine faith, people who were honourable and possessed of a sense of duty. People in whom the light really shone. My objections, my real objections, were doctrinal.

Quite by chance, but also as a result of my family origins, the first such Christian circles that I came across were Protestant. I didn't really get to know them all that well, but when you enter a house, you pick up its smell—one that the occupants have long ago ceased to notice. Similarly, in the speech and example of certain pastors I sensed that the prevailing moralism was rather burdensome and oppressive, but I attempted to get straight to what was essential—a word, the Word for naked man faced with naked death. Yet with them everything focused on a conventionalized understanding of man's encounter with God, of being dazzled by faith, a Kierkegaardian leap. There was a would-be liberating disregard for the sacred that allowed people and things to carry on existing in their secular opacity. From everyone was expected an extremely demanding level of responsibility. In lay circles, morality was an arbitrary imperative founded on a basis of nothingness; but here it stemmed from an anxious desire to be faithful.

What was lacking was the "Eastern" dimension: the mystery of the cosmos and of *eros*, God's radiation even unto the flesh, the lived pulsation of the Spirit. The Will merely skates on the surface of being so, not surprisingly, cases of psychological dissociation seemed to be frequent.[3] It was the period of Barthism of the most classic kind. Barth had not yet expressed his affection for creation. He passionately set faith in opposition to religion, seeing in "religions" nothing but an impotent striving of man towards God, which is truly to commit a gross error. He ignored both the sacramentality of being and man's genuine freedom, which is why the trend in Protestant theology would subsequently be completely reversed, going from a total crushing of the individual to a primary concern for collective freedom, and from the unique glory of the Eternal One to

---

[3] Presumably a refutation of Schopenhauer's assertion that the Will constitutes the innermost essence of things.

a proclamation of the death of God. So many violent oscillations in a sorry search for divine-humanity!

I was attracted, conversely, by the vitality of Catholicism; that is, by the popular form of the religion and by certain examples of holiness. Time and again I would by chance go into a church and, with tears in my eyes, hear the humble congregation replying to the priest as he intoned the first half of the Ave Maria.[4] Protestantism is far too neglectful of this feminine approach to the mystery, which is why its women wish to become pastors, and do so become. "Mother, you at least will not reject us! You at least will not abandon us!" I recalled the way in which God speaks of himself in Isaiah: "'Will a woman forget her child, so as not to have mercy on the offspring of her womb? But even if a woman should forget these things, nevertheless, I shall not forget you,' says the Lord."[5]

I was deeply moved by the photographs of Father Charles Foucauld that I came across. They were taken at different periods in his life, and the transformation accomplished by death that I had seen on certain faces was here taking place whilst he was still fully alive. Whilst still alive, he was passing through fire towards a kind of death-resurrection. Whereas I was shocked by the insipid triviality, the ugliness, of Catholic liturgical art—and much could be said about this catastrophe of beauty—these photos, in which Father Charles's flesh was replaced by glowing embers, were for me

---

[4] When the rosary is recited publicly in church (traditionally before or after daily Mass in the months of May and October), the priest intones the first half of the prayer, the congregation taking up the second half. Strictly speaking, this is true only for the first, third and fifth decade, the roles being reversed in the second and fourth.

[5] Is 49:15–16.

an introduction to the art and theology of the icon. This was something I was shortly to discover, though the icon I had bought must already have secretly been guiding me. These photos were also a response to India and the Far East. When a sage over there reaches the state of awakening, he closes his eyes and savours an all-encompassing enstasy. His face becomes smooth, replete, but inaccessible. On the other hand, when a Christian saint is enlightened, he calls out *abba*, Father, praying as if for the very first time. He enters a state that is always new, always a first time, as it were. He becomes all flame.

I must stress that what prevented me from becoming a Christian at the time I am writing about was the absence, as it seemed to me, of a genuine theology of freedom as well as of any real theology of the Holy Spirit, of any actual experience of the Holy Spirit. The Calvinist doctrine of predestination—which can already be found in St Augustine—filled me with horror. And when I say horror I am not referring simply to my own subjective assessment. I was already reading the Bible and had been influenced by Berdyaev, as I have already said. I was also discovering the Fathers and the Byzantine spiritual masters, above all Irenaeus of Lyons, Dionysius the Areopagite, Maximus the Confessor and Nicolas Cabasilas, as well as all the major writings cited by Vladimir Lossky in his *The Mystical Theology of the Eastern Church*. In short, I was beginning to assimilate the Good News, so when I speak of horror it was clearly not just a personal reaction on my part. Yes, all those arguments concerning free will and grace horrified me. Man always seemed to emerge as nothing more than a puppet. The risk taken by God was nowhere mentioned. The fact that Barth, in one last exhausted attempt to refine things, should have transformed the doctrine of predestination into an assurance of universal salvation—Jesus alone, as it were, being damned—didn't seem to me to change much. Man was still a puppet. The approach of the Jesuits to the question of free will did not convince me either. It seemed merely to focus on the sort of freedom fit for society people, for courtiers who do not call into question the all-powerfulness of the king. Genuine freedom is a far more tragic affair, regal in a different way: for God humbled himself before her, even unto death on the cross. The idea of individual salvation, of a particular judgment for oneself and eternal hell for others—at least, the "objective" discourse of the theologians (which very fact makes it pharisaic)—yes, all of it filled me with horror, just as the same conception of hell had horrified Péguy, marked as he was by the "communionism" of the social movement. An all-powerful God who could create man in full knowledge of the future, and who might turn away from him in the end, abandoning him—given that hell was defined as the offended withdrawal of God—such a God horrified me.

As for the Anselmian conception of redemption—outdated, out of fashion, you will say, and yet it is deeply engrained in the collective sensibility—this necessary immolation of the Son in order to change the mood of the Father (the suffering of a God being needed to appease the anger of a God) well, it seemed to me to be entirely a matter for psychoanalysts.

Did Catholicism convey any better than Protestantism (its more or less illegitimate son) the reality of divine radiance in the Spirit, that real participation in divine life whereby the place of death changes into a place of the Spirit? The Fathers and the Byzantine spiritual masters teach that it is through the Spirit that man in Christ gains knowledge and understanding. Even his body and senses are penetrated by the Spirit, he breathes the Spirit. I tried to read St Thomas Aquinas, but I must confess that he was far too much of a philosopher for me. Like most philosophers, the way he seemed to develop his exposition meant that it unfolded in some exalted sphere that my fundamental lack of philosophical culture prevented me from accessing. I say this not out of any conceited posturing, but rather with a certain sadness. Yet it is a fact that St Thomas did not help me to become a Christian. Nowadays I have come to understand that it is possible to read him not just in the context of Western onto-theology, as Heidegger pejoratively has it, but in that of the Greek Fathers. Only it took me a long time to realize this, and first of all I needed already to have become converted! Be that as it may, I was surprised to find in St Thomas a veritable side-stepping of any language to do with participation—a language which is so evangelical and so Pauline. To become incorporated with the One who contains bodily within himself the fullness of the divinity, to become one being with him, one vine, consanguine. All this language of the body, of the bread of life, of a body which is both eucharistic and ecclesial, all this language of life, of light, of living water—which springs forth from one's innards, as Jesus says, not from the head—I couldn't really see (and I still can't see) how one can account for it by speaking only of a moral, volitional communion, and of grace understood as something that is created. Western Christianity has suffered from theological frigidity—and, as is well known, from frigidity to debauchery is but a small step. It is one that some people take quite cheerfully nowadays.

Then again, I must admit that this story of a Trinity had intrigued me. I had done some reading and had consulted my Catholic and Protestant friends, yet nowhere could I discern such a thing as a Trinity. Simply a bi-unity. They talked all the time about the Father and the Son, and their love for each other. But as for the Holy Spirit, that was just the bond of their love, their sigh of love, their common product. Oh, to be sure, on paper there was an entire doctrine about the Holy Spirit, but I could not see what purpose it served, nor what use the Spirit himself was. The Father and the Son seemed to suffice, which meant that it was difficult not to end up thinking in terms of a theological Oedipus complex!

The Greek Fathers seemed to say something else. More and more studies on them were being published by Catholic authors. There was Jean Daniélou's book on Gregory of Nyssa, those by Urs von Balthasar on Gregory and especially on Maximus the Confessor.[6] These have since counted for a great deal in my life, but I couldn't see any connection, any continuity between the teaching of these Fathers, the Catholic theology of the late Middle Ages and that of modern times. My friends got out of the problem by saying that what the Fathers represented above all was spirituality. But no, that's just it! Their thought was rigorous, yet inseparable from liturgical life, from personal ascesis, and

---

[6] Daniélou's *Grégoire de Nysse : La Vie de Moïse*—translated and introduced by him as the very first volume of the Sources Chrétiennes series—was published by the Éditions du Cerf in 1942. In 1944 came his *Platonisme et théologie mystique: doctrine spirituelle de saint Grégoire de Nysse*, published by Aubier. Urs von Balthasar's *Présence et Pensée: Essai sur la philosophie religieuse de Grégoire de Nysse* was published by Beauchesne in 1942. In 1947 his book on Maximus the Confessor was published by Aubier with the title *Liturgie cosmique*.

from social action. St John Chrysostom composes marvellous homilies on the incomprehensibility of God, concluding by turning to the personal experience of prayer, rooting this in the liturgy, even giving his name to the most frequently celebrated Divine Liturgy in the Byzantine Rite. Yet at the same time he confronts imperial power in the name of freedom of conscience, extensively criticizes the rich, questions the validity of private property and inheritance, and elaborates a plan of social reorganization aimed at eliminating poverty, extending in this way the sacrament of the altar to that of the brother.

Later in the West, everything seems to have fallen apart—with theology on one side, the liturgy on the other, spirituality somewhere else, and the sacrament of the brother consigned to Marxist atheism! Such discordance demoralized me. Among my Catholic friends I discerned, for example, an admirable eucharistic piety. But this was combined with the greatest theological difficulty in being able to give an account of the Eucharist. The Greek Fathers—Cyril of Alexandria, for example, in his commentary on John—never separate the paschal mystery from the transfiguration of the world in Christ and from the very being of the Church as a paschal being, a eucharistic being. Nor indeed from the very being of the world, a world created in order to become Eucharist! All this business about "transubstantiation" seemed to me to be a mediocre metaphysical coup d'État for want, precisely, of any theology of participation. It wasn't the "lost centre", but rather a centre that was partially walled in, trapped and prevented from shining forth with any influence. The same could be said about the way holiness was understood—all the more severe and pure through lacking any theological space.

Since then, Catholicism has begun what one might call the apprenticeship of freedom. Juridical and philosophical structures have collapsed together, and everywhere people are groping about for the living Tradition, though this is something which cannot be externally imposed. So far, and it is a good thing, Catholicism has attempted to come to terms with the Reformation and socialism. Now, I think it is time for it to rediscover Orthodoxy—not as another confession but as its own roots. Only in this way will it be able to combine freedom and mystery.

But I hadn't got that far in my thinking at the time. Catholicism's doctrines had disappointed me, just as today I would have been disappointed by the frequent *absence* of doctrine. I had reached an impasse.

I fumbled and wavered, indecisively. From the exclusivity of Christ as sole mediator, I fell back on India, where all is mediation. My Mediterranean paganism, once rediscovered, expanded ad infinitum. Everything, I suspected, was a game played by God. And so, that gravest of temptations—the one we pray to be delivered from in the final two petitions of the Our Father—wormed its way in, asserted itself. The temptation of false spiritual knowledge, of mystical atheism. The dizzying *I am. I am God*.

Why not, I thought, radically interiorize Christ and Christianity, extracting them from their historical context and simply seeing in them symbols of spiritual fulfilment. Even Berdyaev seemed at times to deviate in this direction. At least, one can read him in this way, if one doesn't know how to situate him properly, how to counterbalance things by placing him in the great tradition of the same Christian East that nurtured him—a tradition that at the time I hardly knew how to make sense of. In the night, strange flashes of inspiration would awaken me. Incarnation, death, resurrection—wasn't this the spiritual destiny of every man, mine too? I am not made in the image of Christ; rather, it is Christ who is my image. Perhaps this was overstating things, but my image, I thought, my own, that of my inner man. That of the Self, just the Self. And so, India was starting to lose its pre-Christian innocence and was becoming anti-Christian, not by rejecting Christ but by assimilating him. Him too, like everything else. So perhaps that was the solution to my problem. Not to reject him, but to assimilate him.

In this, a whole trend of Western thought seemed to agree with me, carried me away, whether it was Nietzsche's Dionysian philosophy, a mystical reading of idealist philosophy, or the magically poetical descriptions of the Übermensch from German Romanticism onwards. Yet this openness to the invisible in which so many Westerners acquiesce nowadays is ambivalent. It is as if the Western psyche were going from petrifaction—as in the various forms of materialism, indeed even in the moralistic, legalistic aspects of recent Christianity—to a sort of liquid state. However, the spirits that breathe upon the waters are not necessarily the Spirit of God. Structuralist philosophers loosen and lift the paving stones on which it seemed natural for us to walk. But what shall we find underneath? Paradise lost? Or perhaps a smoke-filled country bath house full of spiders' webs such as the one to which Svidrigailov compares eternity?[7] When a world delineated by reason and the senses starts to crack, the forces that emerge can just as easily be from "below" as from "above". It is true that, deeper down still, Christ is always present; but when one rejects

---

[7] See Dostoevsky's *Crime and Punishment*, part 4, ch. 1.

him in claiming to assimilate him, is this really a way out of solitude?

An instinctive aversion made me keep my distance from the occult, and from the various techniques that supposedly help one achieve ecstasy, as well as from their caricature as seen in the use of drugs or eroticism. But how many temporary companions did I see crumble to pieces on these twilight paths where nihilism passes itself off as the Absolute!

However, I did experience the same temptation as Kirilov, the character in *The Possessed* in whom Dostoevsky probably embodied the experience of the invisible that he had himself known at the beginning of his crises of epilepsy. Kirilov detached himself from everything, becoming at the same time open to everything, to the point of experiencing eternity in the present moment. As, for example, when he contemplates a leaf that autumn had barely touched, feeling its veins and giving himself over to the point of identifying with the interplay of green and yellow spots.[8] All is good, all is plenitude, the opposition between good and evil no longer exists. Soon he takes things to their logical conclusion and, sovereign master of himself, commits suicide, causing himself to explode into eternity, as it were. The history of humanity, he says, can be divided into two halves: up to Kirilov, the man-monkey; after Kirilov, the man-god. And so, he commits suicide at a moment of his own choosing.

Others who feel the same way would like to destroy everything—society, morality, all Judaeo-Christian constraints—in the hope of gaining access to a state of super-consciousness. This was one of the aspects of the student rebellion of May 1968. Today among certain,

---

[8] A loose allusion to a conversation in part 2, ch. 5.

often quite young, intellectuals the same temptation is introspectively individualized. They pursue, even to the brink of death, that "dissoluteness of all the senses" recommended by Rimbaud.[9] Sometimes they even commit transgressions that include torture and murder—at least in their fantasies. But who knows?

Like Kirilov, I for my part merely preferred my own death. Not suicide as such, directly. That seemed naïve. Kirilov was dead, and then what? Perhaps the very instant of his death still floats in the air, like a bubble of eternity—or soap. Much better, it seemed to me, was an ascesis of indifference—an ascesis, a counter-ascesis, of irresponsibility, of self-annihilation. One evening I was invited to the home of a famous intellectual who collected details of people's spiritual experiences in a very scientific manner, carefully filing them. Later, I realized that he was an aloof, cold individual and tried to "keep warm" as best he could. But there was something terrible about his wife. At a certain point in the evening they began to rail against Christians—people who could not envisage eternity, they said, without the sheep of the Christmas crib. To my shame, I made noises of agreement. They were both well informed about Asiatic spirituality and the wife suddenly said, "In my opinion, spiritual life can be summed up in one phrase: 'Let everything be annihilated'".

There she was, an unfeeling, languorous praying mantis that dreamed of gobbling up not just her husband but the whole world, and God too.

---

[9] "The point is to arrive at the unknown by the dissoluteness of all the senses", from a letter written in 1871 which, together with a few others, constitutes Rimbaud's poetic manifesto. These are known collectively as "The Letters 'of the Visionary'".

And so in order to be everything, I tried to be nothing. I abandoned all responsibility. I was nothing, so I was not responsible. We are all phantoms. I myself do not exist. Since I don't exist, I am but a phantom of the Self. We are all phantoms, ants. How, I wondered, do people manage to put on identities every morning without anxiety? How do they manage to go home again every evening without the least feeling of uncertainty? Especially now that they think they have discovered for the first time certain erotic positions—ones that India has long depicted on its temple walls—that allow them to make love without embracing. Distant from each other, each lost in the void, in the all …

More than anything I wanted to be a sandwich man, a human billboard—the most anonymous job there is. They never look at your face, just the writing that you are carrying round. It is not common knowledge that social outcasts, the downtrodden, often show great affection, though it can quickly turn into cruelty. But what does it matter since everything is the same. I would give them my clothing or the bit of money I had on me. At other times, I was robbed. What did it matter since everything is the same. I liked to sit on the metro steps next to some nameless being. If I went into a restaurant and someone came to serve me, I was bewildered to the point of shedding tears. So they really thought I existed!

One evening I sat looking for a long time—a very long time—at the grain of my wooden table. Everything was there, and all was for the good. Kirilov had been right. When crossing the street, I no longer bothered taking care to avoid the traffic. To be nothing, to be everything, it's all the same. Then I started to go out specifically in order to ignore the traffic even more so, on purpose. And then … then someone looked at me.

It was him, the one in the icon. I shan't claim to have had a visionary experience. There was only silence, words in the silence. But it was his silence, his words, coming from a depth far deeper than that of the Self, a depth where I was no longer alone. He told me that I did exist, that he wanted me to exist, and that I was not nothing. He told me that I was not everything either, but that I *was* responsible. He told me that evil did exist and that it was what I was doing but that, deeper still, he was there. He told me that I needed to be forgiven, healed and recreated. And that in him I *could* be forgiven, healed, and recreated.

"Behold, I stand at the door and knock."[10]

So I opened it.

✥

"I stand at the door and knock."

Higher than our highest joy, he is there. Higher than the "things above" that Dionysius the Areopagite speaks of.[11] And deeper than our despair, for "even the man who desires the very worst life, as wholly desirous of life and that which seems best to him, by the very fact of desiring, and desiring life, and looking to a best life, participates in the Good".[12]

He is lower, turning our very anxiety into trust. And higher, so that our creative freedom finds in the Spirit a space that is infinite.

In the presence of the Disfigured One—the Face of the Father's sacrificial love—the Crucified One from whose pierced side arises the dawn of the Spirit, who

---

[10] Rev. 3:20.
[11] *Celestial Hierarchies*, ch. 1, §1.
[12] *Treatise on the Divine Names*, ch. 4, §20.

would dare speak of a sadistic father or of a master-slave relationship?

Before the Transfigured One whose light permeates humanity and the cosmos, confronted with the liberating Father who gives us the Spirit so that man might become a living being, who would dare define transcendence in terms of castration or death?

Faced with life in Christ, in the Spirit "who searches all things, yes, the deep things of God",[13] who would dare claim that Christianity has lost the keys to knowledge, to love as knowledge, beauty as knowledge, not-knowing as knowledge? For Christianity offers the *supreme identity*[14] without forfeiting difference, which is in fact revealed as being at the heart of the divine.

Unknown Christianity! The newness of Christianity!

God died in the flesh so that man might be resurrected, so that the flesh might be resurrected.

> I believe in the resurrection of the flesh.
> And henceforth
> Deep inside man
> Without fusion or separation,
> In the incandescence of things,
> Without confusion, for the Eucharist,
> In the cry of the Job of history,
> (But God himself becomes a Job
> And leaven of liberation),
> In the desert of transcendence
> Which flowers again in thy blood,
> In the Face of faces,

---

[13] 1 Cor 2:10.
[14] A Hindu concept. The realization of the *supreme identity*—i.e. of *atman* (one's true self) with *brahman* (the Universal Soul)—constitutes Hinduism's understanding of the true end of man. This is something he had discussed at greater length in Chapter 4; see especially page 102.

Disfigured, transfiguring,
We praise thee, we give thee thanks,
O many-hued Wisdom,
O Breath that gives life to all
O Christ who reunifies all,
O abyss at last revealed,
Source of all love, of all freedom,
Abba, the bosom of the Father!
Ecce homo! Behold, the man!

With Christ's death, the crown of thorns of his earthly existence becomes, downwind of the Paraclete, a crown of flames. Man recovers his divine dimension, his all-encompassing humanity, his cosmic vastness. In Christ there exists again but one man. And the cosmos is both humanity's body and a language spoken between God and men, the original Bible. Behold, the man! King, priest and prophet. A king on account of his spiritual dominion over nature: head above, entrails below, and in the centre the sun of the heart where divine energy blazes. A king by virtue of a dominion over the universe that finds expression not in destruction but in communion, and in deference to all life so that it may fully develop. "Blessed are the meek for they shall inherit the earth", though they do so already in the dispossession of their sacrificial offerings. A king by being actively present in history, working in favour of peace and justice—a crucified yet liberating presence which breaks the chain of events surrounding domination and death, and which destroys all forms of slavery whether internal or external. And by displaying a kingly love in which, by an ever-renewed struggle, the life-giving cross asserts itself to be as efficacious as one's lifeblood, as the life force itself.

It is a kingship that goes hand in hand with priestly offerings. As priest, man breathes God, breathes the

Spirit, and thus makes the universe and history breathe God too, sowing in them seeds of eternity. This breathing which is simultaneously prayer, this capacity for "giving thanks in all things",[15] relentlessly and irresistibly draws human knowledge and capability towards the establishing of a communion of persons and the transfiguring of the earth.

Thus man is also a prophet, a prophet of the Resurrection, a prophet of the End that is already present at the heart of the world, undermining its pride and consolidating it in that glory and honour that, according to Revelation, shall enter the new Jerusalem.[16] He is a prophet in the respect he pays to all flesh, since God himself was made flesh, and to every face, since God put on a face. A prophet, too, in the never-ending oscillation between a divine-humanity that is ever to be reinvented and the already ultimate witness of the martyrs: "Give your blood and receive the Spirit".[17]

And so I could no longer avoid the question: this Resurrected One who resurrects us in turn, where was he to be found? Where could one unite oneself to him so as to become "one body" and "one blood"? Admittedly, Christ is everywhere present, attracting to himself human history and the future evolution of the universe. As Nicolas of Cusa said, he is the Maximum Man. But the Jesus of history is simply a Christ who is "re-crucified". It was for the Resurrected One that I thirsted. It is also true that Christ gives himself in his Word, and I was now hardly ever parted from my

---

[15] Eph 5:20.
[16] Rev 21:26: "And they shall bring the glory and the honour of the nations into [Jerusalem]."
[17] An adaptation of a saying by Abba Longinus; see *The Sayings of the Desert Fathers: The Alphabetical Collection*, trans. Benedicta Ward (London & Oxford: Mowbrays, 1975), 104.

New Testament and the Gospels. But the Word was made flesh, and it was for this flesh that I hungered. I couldn't get out of my mind the episode in John's Gospel concerning the "bread of life". "Amen, amen, I say to you, unless you eat the flesh of the Son of Man and drink his blood, you have no life in you. Whoever eats My flesh and drinks My blood has eternal life, and I will raise him up on the last day. For My flesh is food indeed, and My blood is drink indeed. He who eats My flesh and drinks My blood abides in Me, and I in him."[18] I was fiercely opposed to any spiritualistic interpretation of this text. *Ho trogon mou tēn sarka*: "he who eats my flesh". There is nothing spiritualistic about the verb *trogein*!

I was hungry for the Eucharist.

I was hungry for a Church that was first and foremost Eucharist. For a community that confessed itself to be—above and beyond all sociology—the Body of Christ in the Eucharist. For a theology that came from the eucharistic chalice.

It was at this point that I met certain Orthodox.

---

[18] Jn 6:53–6.

✧ 7 ✧

Lossky, Father Sophrony, Evdokimov

Curiously, neither my reading of Berdyaev nor my purchase of an icon had made me aware that there was such a thing as the Orthodox Church. For me, being a Christian had meant being a Catholic or a Protestant.

Yet I remember that there was a certain man I had got to know among the *Cheval blanc* community. He was kind and gentle, with a somewhat wry sense of humour. Like me, he was ill at ease with the hothouse atmosphere during the intense chatter of the "collective". He has since published several fine books that have gone almost unnoticed and has pursued a useful career overseas with Unesco, helping to protect ancient monuments of beauty from the mania of modernism. One day, during one of the worst moments, he said to me, "You will be Russian. You will be Byzantine". (He had an understanding—and it is a rare thing—of the spiritual grandeur of Byzantium.) He meant Orthodox. However, he was not altogether wrong. Many years later Paul Evdokimov in one of his books included me—last offspring, runt,[1] or graft,

---

[1] This is the word (*avorton*) used in French translations of 1 Cor 15:8, where Paul is describing himself as the last and least of the apostles.

rather—among the Russian religious philosophers! It was absurd, and I told him so. He knew it was, but simply smiled. The Russian religious philosophers were promoters of encounter—between the Christian West and East, between Christianity and modernity. I don't object to this filiation; it has led me to others, for which Paul Evdokimov paved the way: Christian Hellenism, for example, and Semitic Christianity. When I listen to Metropolitan Meliton of Chalcedon or to Metropolitan Maximus of Sardis, it is the maternal voice of spiritual Byzantium that I hear. And when I listen to Georges Khodr, it is the original voice of the Bible that captivates me. Filiations? What counts is to find the main focus and that for me, after all, is my French filiation. But that is a rather complex matter, to which I shall return.

"You will be Russian." I have already mentioned Berdyaev, and I have repeatedly quoted Dostoevsky. When I first came across the episode in *Crime and Punishment* where a murderer [Raskolnikov] and a prostitute [Sonia] together read the Gospel passage recounting the resurrection of Lazarus, it had seemed to me that, for the first time with this book, a definitive word had been spoken. The Word had been proclaimed to the atheists of today.

"*And he that was dead came forth.*

She read loudly, cold and trembling with ecstasy, as though she were seeing it before her eyes."[2]

And he that was dead came forth.

A word proclaimed to naked man faced with naked death. The New Testament that Sonia was reading from had been Lizaveta's—the very person Raskol-

---

[2] See part 4, ch. 4 of Dostoevsky's *Crime and Punishment*, trans. Constance Garnett (London: Heinemann, 1914), 289–91.

nikov had murdered, despite himself. Without wanting to: a naked death, a blind death.
"Jesus said unto her, *I am the resurrection and the life. Believest thou this*? And drawing a painful breath, Sonia read distinctly and forcibly as though she were making a public confession of faith. 'Yea, Lord'."

Recently I saw a dramatization of this novel in a Parisian theatre. The audience was full of young people and I noticed that they held their breath as certain words struck at their core. After all, the Orthodox are the only Christians to have given to modernism one of modernism's fathers. Dostoevsky is just as important as the others—the Marxes, the Freuds and the Nietzsches. Even more important, in the final analysis. We must take up again that saying of Berdyaev that I have already quoted, restate it, make it known, almost as a duty: Dostoevsky knew all that others knew, with something added. Someone, rather. To wish to talk about Christ today without knowing what these others knew seems to me to be futile. But to know what the others knew without having met Christ is not to progress very far either.

✢

The Russian Orthodox whom I met at that time were basically engaged in bringing about an encounter between Orthodoxy and France. I had read Vladimir Lossky's *Essai sur la théologie mystique de l'Église d'Orient* several times, so I decided to seek him out. In doing so I had to navigate my way through several small, friendly, but oppressive circles in which Orthodoxy had been made into a battle flag. I had already been acquainted with quite a few circles of this kind and they didn't appeal to me much—though I am perhaps being unfair as to what these Orthodox were trying to achieve. Be that as it may, after being an activist himself in one of these groups, Lossky ceased to be a member—for very good canonical reasons. (He didn't treat such things lightly, considering that the canons are to the Church what asceticism is to the individual.) But he left above all because he felt that for him the time had come for subtlety and serenity rather than polemics and proselytism, attitudes which are anyway so foreign to the fundamental genius of Orthodoxy. I followed him. It was he who taught me theology.

Vladimir Lossky was from Petersburg, the most European city in Russia, one that seems to have come straight out of a painting by Claude Lorrain. Later I would find myself strolling up and down the banks of the River Neva in his company, as he recounted his childhood memories. Strangely enough, he too had been haunted by death. He told me how he had put his chaplain on the spot with regard to God's omnipotence by asking him whether God was able to create a stone so heavy that he would be unable to lift it! "Now," he told me, "I know the answer. That stone is man."

In the long, late August twilights when the sky in this delta city mingles so effortlessly with the water, Lossky and Dimitri Obolensky would recite poems to each other in a state of euphoria:

> The heavy Neva is in the huge room
> And light blue blood streams out
> of the granite.[3]

---

[3] Lines from Osip Mandelstam's 1916 poem, "Solominka", as translated by Clarence Brown; see C. Brown, *Mandelstam* (London: Cambridge University Press, 1973), 239. Sir Dimitri Obolensky (1918–2001) was a Russian-born historian who settled in Britain and became Professor of Russian and Balkan History at the University of Oxford. His most important book was *The Byzantine Commonwealth* (1971), a large-scale

Walking by their side, I gained an understanding of how Petersburg had been a dream created by force, but that this force had dissipated—not as city but as civilization. At the heart of this capital city—last chef d'œuvre of European monarchical architecture—Falconet erected an equestrian statue of Peter the Great. Its pedestal is a giant glacial block of granite that had been dragged here by serfs over many years across the bogs of Finland. Reared up, the horse confronts a serpent. In a poem that Lossky quoted to me at the foot of this statue, Alexander Blok prophesied that the serpent would be victorious.[4] The peat lands of Finland have been burnt up and the horse and Russia of Peter have indeed collapsed, leaving a civilization full of cracks whose breakdown was made inevitable by the First World War. In the early twentieth century, however, it was a civilization that had attained a high level of creative power in many cultural areas, and a genuine universality as well.

Vladimir Lossky was the son of the important philosopher Nikolay Lossky, who was associated with the Russian Religious Renaissance.[5] His own studies had already caused him to lean towards the West, for the University of Petersburg specialized, among other

> synthesis of the history of the Eastern Roman Empire. In 1988 he returned to Russia as a delegate to the Sobor or Council of the Russian Orthodox Church, convoked to celebrate the 1,000th anniversary of the conversion of Russia. Among his many other achievements he edited, with an introduction and prose translations, *The Penguin Book of Russian Verse*.

[4] Presumably a reference to the controversial poem entitled *The Twelve*.

[5] The phrase brings to mind the title of an important 1963 book by Nicholas Zernov, *The Russian Religious Renaissance of the Twentieth Century* (London: Darton, Longman & Todd). The period concerned dates roughly from 1880 to 1950.

things, in the Western Middle Ages. Born in 1903 and barely an adolescent when the Revolution came, he had been exiled along with his father in that famous year of 1922 when all major non-Marxist intellectuals were banished. Soon, he found himself in Paris, definitively integrated into French life. As a student of Étienne Gilson at the Sorbonne, he was able to get back to his beloved Western Middle Ages. When I got to know him, he was engaged in academic research. True, this was after years of genuine hardship that I believe he endured with a fair amount of indifference. He collaborated with the editorial team responsible for the journal *Dieu vivant*, lectured at the Collège philosophique, and broke lances with the major theologians of the Catholic patristic revival at the same time as getting on marvellously with them.[6] With very few exceptions, he wrote his articles and books directly in French, and when his thought was serene it had a crystal-clear precision about it. Even during the period when he militated on behalf of a diehard Orthodoxy, he had spent almost every day—to the despair of the fanatics—drafting a thesis on Meister Eckhart, the great fourteenth-century Rhenan mystic, continually rewriting it. Most probably because he could not bring himself to part company with him. I edited the manuscript after his premature death.[7] He venerated St Francis of Assisi and also took me on pilgrimage to

---

[6] For further, highly interesting, information concerning these encounters, see the text written by Lossky's elder son, Father Nicholas, and published as an Appendix to Vladimir Lossky, trans. and annotated by Michael Donley *Seven Days on the Roads of France: June 1940* (Crestwood, NY: St Vladimir's Seminary Press, 2012), 110.

[7] Vladimir Lossky, *Théologie négative et connaissance de Dieu chez Maitre Eckhart* (Paris: Vrin, 1960).

La Salette.[8] I don't believe I gave him more pleasure than on a certain Christmas Day, when I gave him a collection of reproductions of miniatures painted on manuscripts of the Minnesänger. Reserved as he was and despite his horror of Russian pathos, he stood up and embraced me! He had married a kind-hearted, intelligent Jewish woman who had become converted to Christianity. In the metro she would read the Bible, or Shakespeare in the original. Lossky himself would read the entire Bible during Lent, from Genesis to Revelation. Theirs was an ever open house.

Lossky was firmly rooted in the Church, like a tree in nutritive soil. It was through him to begin with, through his family circle, and through the life of the small parish of which he was a member (where services were held in Slavonic at first, then little by little in French) that I discovered the Church not as morality, ideology or a social and political force but as liturgical, eucharistic humus in which man is nourished and transformed.[9] That is, the inner man, starting with the heart and then spreading to one's entire being, asceticism simply being a way of removing obstacles that get in the way of this great rising of sap.

Once I had made this discovery, I have never had a problem with the Church. On the contrary, its necessity has become ever more clear to me. For, in truth, the Church is nothing other than the Eucharist, the sacramental Body of Christ where the Spirit abounds: "Whoever eats my flesh and drinks my blood has eter-

---

[8] For the importance to Lossky of La Salette, see *Seven Days*, 42–4, especially notes 10 and 12.

[9] The parish in question is that of Our Lady Joy of All who Sorrow and St Genevieve, rue Saint Victor, Paris VII.

nal life."[10] In the Eucharist, says St Nicholas Cabasilas, we find life at its highest degree of intensity. So from then on I realized that the celebration of an encounter, the friendly meal, the struggle for justice and liberty, techniques of concentration, the deepening of existence by beauty, and the serious exercise of thought, far from being an alternative to the Eucharist find in it their eternal depth.

Lossky was squarely rooted in this soil. Even his hospitality, which was so magnanimous, had something ecclesial about it. Often it took the form of veritable *agapes*, extending and multiplying the eucharistic celebration. Sometimes these would begin in a bistro. During the vigil service on Saturday evenings when at a certain point the Church is in darkness, save for the light of the tapers and the oil-lamps beneath the icons, Lossky would read the Six Psalms in a somewhat gravelly voice but without affectation. Stocky, bolt upright, like a knight of the Invisible.

In the plane taking us to Moscow,[11] without intending to, I caught him telling his beads—that is, saying the Jesus Prayer, the sinews of the hesychast "method". He wasn't using a monastic prayer rope either, the sort usually made of leather or wool, but a small set of Catholic rosary beads of black wood. A few minutes later, he said to me, "You know, the ecclesiastical circles over there will be rather ponderous, so I've brought Apollinaire's *Alcools* with me". For he loved the kind

---

[10] Jn 6:54.
[11] In August 1956. Along with Lossky, Obolensky and Clément went Hieromonk Basil Krivoshein (future Archbishop of Brussels and Belgium), noted for his pioneering books on St Symeon the New Theologian. In September of the same year, Lossky wrote a moving letter to his father about this visit. This is reproduced in his *Seven Days*, 96–8.

of poetry that sang for the sake of singing, without too many metaphysical pretensions.[12] He knew what sort of men his bishops were, which did not stop him respecting them, even and above all when he disagreed with them. It is the Eucharist that postulates the bishop, who is the witness of God's faithfulness. When all the faithful ask the Father to send his Spirit upon the congregation, on the bread and wine, in order to incorporate all into the Body of Christ, they know they are not "waiting for Godot" — precisely because of the witness and apostolic presence of the bishop.

Vladimir Lossky felt he had a mission based on a spiritual interpretation of contemporary history. The suffering, indeed the agony, that the Russian Church was experiencing — and which has undoubtedly given more martyrs in this twentieth century than the whole of Christianity in its previous history — together with the associated dispersal of so many Orthodox was in his opinion providential, since it had brought about an in-depth encounter between Christians of the East and the West. Of this encounter he was himself the very embodiment. To begin with, as mentioned, he had conceived things in terms of proselytism and conversion, but by the time I knew him he had come to believe that, through the test of exile, Orthodoxy must first of all become converted to its own universality so as to detect and in all humility foster germs of unity

---

[12] The contrast between this particular volume and the context in which Lossky would be reading it is brought out once one becomes aware of the poet's highly unconventional background. Guillaume Apollinaire (1880–1918) was a forerunner of surrealism and is even credited with coining the very terms "cubism" and "surrealism". Despite its modernism, *Alcools* does contain several poems which are imbued with Arthurian legend — something which would have appealed to Lossky, given his interest in the Middle Ages.

within Western Christianity. His monumental, unfinished thesis on Meister Eckhart is exemplary of this loving knowledge. He was a creative writer who was not content merely to systematize the teaching of the Fathers—though he did so brilliantly—but who also attempted to address problems of the day. His calling into question Roman Catholicism's theology of the Spirit, even though it underestimated Latin patristics, had something salubrious about it. It was a spur to making progress.

Lossky knew he would die young. He suffered from a heart defect that had been aggravated by the winters without heating during the Revolution and the Civil War. He knew that he might die at any moment. Yet he had a sociable side, but became more and more detached and by that very fact more and more open to people and things. One 2nd of November, tired of seeing so many chrysanthemums for the dead,[13] he presented my wife with a bunch of roses, saying, "I bring flowers to the living. There are only the living!" A few days before his death, he had a dream about his own corpse, but reflected on it quite calmly. He died very quickly, aged 55. Most of his books appeared posthumously. I helped in getting them published.

Though only ever inspired by Tradition, Vladimir Lossky was a creative thinker. This is especially true of the way he presented the theological understanding of the *person*. In fact, it was this that enabled me fully to embrace the mystery of a personal God. I had been torn between the Hindu sense of total but transpersonal identity and the European sense of an *I* and a *Thou* that were unique but merely similar; but all this was resolved by the revelation of the Tri-unity,

---

[13] See page 71, note 2, for clarification of this custom.

which is itself the key to the revelation of man. For, as Lossky emphasized, it was precisely during the great elaborations of Trinitarian theology that the idea of personhood originated, becoming the driving force and stumbling block of world history. The Fathers liked to contrast the mystery of the Trinity with the closed transcendence of Judaism as well as with the polytheistic immanence of paganism. Nowadays, I used to say to Lossky, I would rather discern in it the surpassing and integration, on the one hand, of the transpersonal abyss of the mystics of absorption as well as, on the other, the divisive individualism of the evidently post-Christian West. Lossky insisted that the Trinity should in no sense be thought of in binary terms—the One opening itself up and then closing again—for that would still be based on human rationality. In the "meta-mathematics" of the Trinity, the mysterious Third Person, the Spirit, does not simply ensure the unity of the One and the Other, the Father and the Son. He signifies the infinite surpassing of all opposition, not by a simple return to the origin but by affirming absolute diversity in absolute unity. The Tri-unity is thus a more total unity than that of India for, in the Spirit, it simultaneously contains absolute identicalness and absolute difference in such a way that difference is no longer separation but an ineffably unique mode of this unity's existence. Here the Person is no longer an individual who fragments and opposes, but the concurrence—though this is inconceivable for reason and gnosis alike—of difference and non-difference, of "distinctions" and "unions", to use the terms of Dionysius the Areopagite. The Persons are not fractions of the whole; they contain and communicate the whole. They contain each other mutually and without confusion. The Absolute is not above and beyond the Persons; it constitutes their depth, their transparency and the dynamism of their communion.

In Christ, inspired by the fire of the Spirit, humanity already partakes secretly in this great Trinitarian rhythm; we are each called to partake in it consciously. In the formulations of Lossky and the Greek Fathers, I recognized the powerful (yet so undeveloped) vision of the socialist Pierre Leroux: all human beings are like the Trinity![14] All human beings, across time and space, constitute a single man in the most realistic sense, all are one body, "members of one another", in St Paul's phrase,[15] in the Maximum Man, the God-Man who imparts to them Trinitarian life. Each is responsible for all. Salvation is not an individual matter but personal; that is, communal. Lossky, like the Romanian theologian Dumitru Staniloae at the same period, revived that admirable theology of communion that is based on the Palamite distinction between God's essence and his energies. In order to deal with rationalist "reductionism" and "demythologizing", St Gregory Palamas (the fourteenth-century Greek theologian) was motivated to work out a theology of life in Christ and the lived experience of the Holy Spirit. Though God is inaccessible in his essence, he says, he freely gives himself in his energies. By "energy" is meant both a personal action producing an encounter that invites one to communion and also a powerful radiation of Light that, within this communion, becomes capable of being participated in. God is totally inaccessible, says Palamas, but makes himself totally participable, even as he is veiled by the very profusion of his light, all the

---

[14] See page 18.
[15] Rom 12:5; Eph 4:25.

more unknown in being known. Palamas applied this "distinction-identicalness"[16] to man as well for, since we are each made in the image of the Unknowable, we are ourselves unknowable, except insofar as we radiate a creative love that has been set free from all separation and death by the very radiation of God. In Lossky we find the crucial idea that the *person* is the irreducibility of man to his nature. In the flowing stream of the divine energies, man discovers his identicalness with all men at the same time as becoming, without seeking it, entirely unique and incomparable.

And so, I was delivered from the temptation of madness. It was Lossky who introduced me to the terrible saying of Paul Florensky that humanity would have no other choice, in the final analysis, than between the Trinity and madness.[17]

Madness, the pernicious loneliness of the contemporary West, the incommunicability of individuals who are merely similar (just enough to be able to cause each other pain and suffering), each walled in by his wish to do his own will, in the opacity of the self. In other words, walled in by nothingness, that secret screen onto which our civilization projects its fantasies.

Madness, those intense experiences into which this very loneliness throws individuals: totalitarian politics, eroticism, drugs or an incestuous return to the womb of the mother or the earth, or death.

---

[16] This expression, coined by Lossky, uses the term *identité* in the sense of "sameness" or, as we have preferred to render it, "identicalness".

[17] "We are free to choose, but we must decide either on the one or on the other: either the search for the Trinity or the dying in madness ... *Tertium non datur!*" See P. Florensky, *The Pillar and Ground of the Truth*, trans. Boris Jakim (Princeton: Princeton University Press, 2004), 49.

Madness (at least for the westerner of today who gets bogged down in them), the religions of Asia, in which loneliness becomes absolute. And there is not a single person on the planet who does not have something of the West in him nowadays, even if filtered through Marxism, and who has thus been influenced — however little, however unconsciously — by the Gospel's call to personal responsibility.

Only the doctrine of the Tri-Unity, re-expressed in a revolutionary manner in the way that Lossky had begun to do, can cure this madness and allow man to become, without separation or confusion, a person existing in communion, embracing and offering back to God the whole of humanity and the universe.

When I discussed the diversity of religions with Vladimir Lossky, he drew my attention to those texts of St Maximus the Confessor in which he refers to the three "incarnations" of the Logos, the Word and Wisdom of God: a cosmic incarnation in the spiritual essences of things that the sage gathers and offers, as in the best of the ancient traditions of India; an incarnation in the Law when, with the calling of Abraham and then the covenant with Moses, a history of salvation emerges — and this is the significance of the "religions of the Book", Judaism and Islam;[18] and thirdly, there is Christ, who is also the origin of all and who thus recapitulates, restores and fulfils the meaning of both the universe and of history.

✢

---

[18] It is noteworthy that Clément avoids the common mistake of including Christianity as one of the "religions of the Book". It is above all else the "religion of a Person".

It was Lossky who introduced me to Father Sophrony, and in him Mount Athos.

A young intellectual cast up on the shores of the West by the revolutionary turmoil like so many others, the future monk Sophrony began a career as a painter in Paris but suddenly sacrificed his artistic talents and set off for Athos. Though at first unsettled, he became the spiritual son and then the friend and confidant of one of the greatest mystics of the twentieth century, *Starets* Silouan. After the latter's death in 1938, Father Sophrony inherited his notebooks and became more and more convinced that he ought to convey Silouan's message to the wider world in a way that would allow it to reveal its full force. To convey, to make known this word that is of such humility and such simplicity that it does not exist in and of itself but becomes, as at times does the sea that washes the coast of the Holy Mountain, pure transparency. It is a word that is transparent to universal love in such a way that the real relationship between a monk and the world becomes evident: the monk becomes the world's transparency to the divine energies, energies that as a cross-bearer he discerns even in the netherworld of his being.

Silouan was a Russian peasant who, before arriving on Athos, had known only his own village, yet he carried in his prayers all men, the whole of humanity including India and China. All outcasts, all the lost. Especially those who persecuted the Church, for he believed that the only proof that one was walking in Christ, towards Christ, was this evangelical love for one's enemies. He himself had gone through hell. Not only because, when quite young, he had become involved in a brawl and had accidentally all but killed a man but also because, shortly after his admission to the monastery, he had been cast into the abyss for having wished to savour and, as it were, cling to his first experiences of spiritual bliss. And there, amid his anguish and despair, he had met Christ, who said to him, "Keep your mind in hell, and do not despair".

At the time I met Father Sophrony he was living at Sainte-Geneviève-des-Bois in the so-called "donjon", the large round tower, of the dilapidated Château.[19] He had converted it himself with that skill reminiscent of the resourcefulness of a Ulysses that Athonite monks possess, so accustomed are they to carrying out all kinds of manual tasks. Without specializing in any, for the monk is interested in everything without restricting himself to one thing. He constantly seeks the relationship of things—not just between each other but between them and the invisible. Father Sophrony had

---

[19] The château de la Cossonerie has a fascinating history. It was bought shortly after the First World War by a rich English eccentric, Miss Dorothy Paget, specifically for Princess Vera Meshchersky. Miss Paget was the daughter of Lord Queenborough and Pauline Whitney, an heiress from the notable American Whitney family. Princess Vera had fled to France after the Revolution and founded in Paris a finishing school for girls, where Dorothy Paget was educated. She became a great friend of the Princess as well as of her niece Olga, and developed a profound interest in the fate of Russian refugees. In 1927, thanks to Dorothy, a home and place of refuge was founded in Sainte-Geneviève-des-Bois, which at the time was still a village. Ironically, the château had at one time belonged to the private secretary of Napoleon Bonaparte, he whose failure to invade Russia is celebrated in Tchaikovsky's 1812 Overture. It was this establishment—which became known as "La Maison Russe"—that was the origin of the Russian colony in the area. Although the château's first inhabitants tended to be White Russians, the buildings were later to welcome other Russians in dire straits, whether from the Soviet Union or Nazi Germany, for example. It still functions today as an old people's home. Dorothy Paget also purchased the plot for the world-famous Russian cemetery. Not surprisingly, in Sainte-Geneviève-des-Bois a street is named after her.

that somewhat brusque vivacity—I mean the sort that is devoid of any cloying sentimentality—that is often found in experienced Athonites. He had left Athos in the aftermath of the Second World War when the repercussions of the Greek revolution and counter-revolution were rife, but also for reasons of health. Thin, lively, with that transparent pallor, especially of the forehead, that with a certain stylization ascetic texts call "yellow" but which makes one think rather of purified earth. The monk is someone who purifies the earth with his body. There was nothing sentimental about him, then, but—why not mention it?—he had the gift of tears. He never spoke to me about this; I discovered it for myself one day, accidentally. "The deep waters of the heart"[20] that flow gently without there being the least contracting or tensing of the face. The *apatheia* of someone who has transformed the power of the passions into a strong but gentle tenderness that is able to sense things in a maternal fashion. "Why were you so sad yesterday?" he once inquired. Now, he had only happened to see me by chance, and from a distance, at some rather crowded meeting during which I had not said anything special. It was the gift of tears that no doubt explained this exceptional sensitivity, this extraordinarily subtle presence among men.

Father Sophrony was an aristocrat of the spirit, with at the same time something of an abrupt, almost haughty, manner—though this could suddenly change to an attitude of welcome. Though he was strict, almost harsh in some cases (which shocked me, but I was wrong), he showed much gentleness in conversation. He never judged, never blamed, and never gave orders.

---

[20] An allusion to Prov 20:5: "Counsel in a man's heart is like deep water, but a prudent man will draw it out."

He would simply refer to such and such a case, known to him or even one that he had himself experienced, and in which a particular solution had proved beneficial. Later, when reflecting on our discussion, I would find myself saying, "But that case ... it's mine too!" I noticed that in his conversation he would jump from one thing to another in an odd way. Years later, he explained to me that when he received anyone, he would try to empty himself, try not to interpose himself, but to open himself to the other and to God. What he did not say was that, in order to arrive at this double emptying, one must have achieved the state of spontaneous prayer that is no longer separated from one's breathing and the beating of one's heart. Then man no longer prays, he has become prayer, and in him is expressed the celebration of the universe. On the altar of his heart, he becomes the priest of the world. Open to the other and to God, and as if emptied of self, a thought emerges from his depths and demands to be spoken, even if it seems incongruous and interrupts the flow of the conversation. It is precisely the word that the other needs, that awakens, that lances a secret abscess, that pacifies, unifies or consoles.

Father Sophrony was not just a master of "the art of arts and the science of sciences", the only specifically Christian counterpart, it seems to me, to the psychosomatic techniques of the East. He also made me understand that Christianity is not an ideology but the Resurrection, and that Christian life is the transforming consciousness of our own resurrection in the Resurrected One. From generation to generation, men have seen Christ—not mediated by this or that, but Christ himself, his beloved Face. From generation to generation, men have communed consciously with the Living One, just as Paul did when he was suddenly bowled over on the road to

Damascus. "The ant must be overturned to be able to see the sky", runs an oriental saying. Like the murdered Stephen praying "do not charge them with this sin"; like John, the serene seer of Patmos. Thus is forged a "golden chain" of apostolic men who can speak of the Living One because they speak of what they know. Father Sophrony used to say that such people, whatever their position in the Church, belong to "the priesthood after the order of Melchizedek".[21] Yet such people, by their humility and prayer, do no more than encapsulate the sacramental, eucharistic experience of the Church—an experience through love and beauty of "heaven on earth", which entitles the people to sing, after communion, "We have seen the true light".

Above all else perhaps, by clarifying my deepest experiences Father Sophrony enabled me to understand what it is that we saved from; namely, hell. Hell is the last place of salvation, as is sung in the Paschal Canon: "All things are now filled with light, heaven and earth, and even the nethermost regions". To know that one is saved from hell, saved whilst *in* hell, to know that the only choice is to be either the thief on the left or the one on the right and to become aware, still being a thief, not just of one's sins in the plural but of a certain state of separation, of failure, of permanent asphyxia—of the very sort that threw me to the ground in the "zone"[22]—all this leads one to a radical humility, to a permanent state of *metanoia*. *Metanoia*, that "reversal" in the way we see the world, that break with the self-idolatry that we project onto others and onto things. "Keep your mind in hell, and do not despair." The incarnate God, the God who endures on

---

[21] Ps 110:4; Heb 5:6.
[22] See page 80.

the cross not just a physical death but a spiritual one, is to be found from now on in the very place of his own absence. For all things are filled with light, even hell.

"Yes," I said, "hell as humanity's condition is abolished, but a person can still imprison himself in himself, even if only in his mind. And isn't that another hell, no longer generic but personal, the 'second death' of which Revelation speaks?"

Father Sophrony gently explained to me that no objective discussion about hell is possible, and that one cannot speak of hell for others. No-one is alone, God abandons no-one, the communion of saints (those pardoned sinners) corrode the walls of that ultimate prison—that of the self enclosed in itself. Universal salvation cannot be thought to be a certainty, for that would empty spiritual life of its seriousness, and human freedom of its tragic grandeur. But it must be the subject of our prayer, of our active love, of our hope. It was in this context that Father Sophrony told me the story of the shoemaker of Alexandria, one that has been transmitted from generation to generation of monks since the fourth century. Anthony the Great, "Father of monks" and athlete of Christ, asked him one day whether or not he was on the right path. "Yes," Christ replied, "you are doing well but in Alexandria there is a shoemaker who is ahead of you." So Anthony went in search of this shoemaker. He introduces himself but the shoemaker throws himself at Anthony's feet, replying that he leads a humdrum life and doesn't know why Anthony thinks he is special. "Perhaps it is this," he then says. "All that I earn I divide into three equal parts, one for those poorer than myself, one for the Church, and one for my family." However, Anthony was not convinced, for he himself had sold all his possessions and distributed the money among the poor, after hearing read in church Jesus' injunction to the rich young man, "You still lack one thing. Sell all that you have and give the money to the poor. Then come and follow me." So Anthony tells the shoemaker what Christ had said to him, and the shoemaker reflects. "Well, perhaps it is this, then. All day long as I am at work I see many, many people passing by. Alexandria is such a big city. So I pray, 'Let them all be saved, I alone deserve to be lost'".

Hell is never for others. And whoever finds himself in hell cannot not meet Christ there.

"But should he refuse to open his heart," I countered, "then hell would be eternal".

"Be sure that Christ is there with him."[23]

✣

Soon I was to meet Paul Evdokimov and to become his friend. He belonged to the same generation as Lossky but, whereas Lossky's destiny had been prematurely cut short, Evdokimov was able to see his work through. Its impact has been profound, if discreet, on those Western Christians who seek a deeper spiritual life. Evdokimov understood people well. He wrote his principal works — directly in French, like Lossky — when he had turned fifty, so they were the fruit of a long period of actual, meaningful service. He had taken part in the civil war but refused to speak about it except when reminiscing, with a smile, about his horse. When they slept in the snow, it would lie around him so as to keep him warm. Then came Constantinople, Paris,

---

[23] In 1958 Elder Sophrony (Sakharov, 1896–1993), the spiritual child and biographer of St Silouan the Athonite, moved to England and founded the Monastery of St John the Baptist at Tolleshunt Knights, Essex. He was canonized himself in 2019 by Patriarch Bartholomew of Constantinople.

loneliness and destitution. He took a series of jobs—cook, worker in an automobile factory, then night worker on the metro tracks so as to be able to study during the day as one of the first students at the newly opened Institut Saint-Serge. Several Russian theologians and religious philosophers founded this between the wars with the aim of combining Tradition with free research. During the Second World War Evdokimov took part in the Resistance in Christian circles, devoting himself to the service of refugees and, together with Protestant friends, was one of the founders of the Cimade [*Comité inter-mouvements auprès des évacués*].[24] In the aftermath of the conflict, he was in charge of a welcome centre for displaced persons. He had the gift of understanding the most deprived of people and of making their life worth living again. Then for a long time he was in charge of a student hostel to which refugees flocked from eastern Europe, Portugal and its colonies, and Brazil. There were also a good number of African scholarship holders. It was in the company of these young men from all over the world that he developed the basic essentials of his writings, as with them he tried to make sense of history in the light of the Spirit.

For him, a page had been turned for good—that of his Russian origins. To be sure, he still harboured, like

[24] The Cimade is a non-governmental organization founded in October 1939 by student groups to give assistance and support to people uprooted by war—in the first instance those who were evacuated from the French provinces of Alsace and Lorraine, located on the border with Germany. Under German occupation the Cimade continued its operations, working with refugees, many of whom were Jewish. Later they were active in underground work that provided protection for Jews in France. Today, they continue their work with uprooted people, especially undocumented immigrants in France.

a nostalgia for paradise, the memory of the monasteries his mother took him to as a child. The gardens, the abundance of melodious bells, the gentle rhythm of the ritual, the joyful crowds ... And also the blessing a *starets* gave him at the very worst moment of the civil war. This was something he told me about at the very end of his life, under the pines and sky of the Mediterranean where we were spending our holidays together. Yet he never saw his duty as being anywhere other than in France, with a view to an encounter that would give back to Christianity its equilibrium and its fullness.

Lossky and Evdokimov: my two teachers, the one more specifically in theology, the other in religious philosophy. Lossky would draw up various structures, albeit open-ended ones, in order to do away with concepts, to crucify them. Thus, distinction-identicalness, unresolved antinomies, the human and the divine in Christ being "without separation or confusion", the meta-mathematics of the Tri-Unity, the essence and the energies. And, especially, the real key to his thought: the distinction between nature and person that enables God to break through the wall of his own transcendence in order to suffer death in the flesh, as the Fifth Ecumenical Council affirms. Around these open-ended structures—provided one avoided the temptation to make them into a closed system—all became limpid, alive, and filled one with admiration for human intelligence. Lossky was one of those who rediscovered not just the spirituality of the Fathers but their doctrine, and not simply their doctrine but their creative spirit.

As for Evdokimov, he was more like a musician and one must know how to read him. His style is full of nuances and reprises that seem disconcerting at first, but that turn out to have contributed to a symphonic whole. One cannot compare it to that crystal-clear and at times solid "castle of the soul"[25] that Lossky constructed; it moves like the tide, ebbing and flowing, and yet one eventually realizes that it is making headway.[26] With Lossky one learns how to think differently, with Evdokimov how to feel differently. His *Ages of the Spiritual Life* has transformed more than one destiny.

It was through Evdokimov that I fully discovered Russian religious philosophy, one of the most fertile encounters to have taken place between Christianity and modernity. It bore its last fruits in France among writers and teachers connected with the Institut Saint-Serge between 1925 and 1950. The idea was to shed light on contemporary culture in a resurgence, as it were, of Pentecost. To discern the Christian meaning of eros, of the cosmos, of beauty, of a creative freedom and of persons in communion.

A religious philosopher is not a philosopher in the sense in which the word is generally understood in Western Europe. Nor is he a theologian, whose task is to deepen our understanding of revelation. The perspective of the religious philosopher is more a matter, as it were, of prophecy. He attempts to interpret everything in the light of revelation. Everything! Whether it be

---

[25] An allusion to St Teresa of Avila's book known in English as *The Interior Castle*. The title *Le Château intérieur* does exist in French, but *Le Château de l'âme* is also commonly used. A combination of these two clarifies the topic of the book as being the "interior castle of the soul". The fact that, in her vision, St Teresa saw the soul as a diamond perhaps explains Clément's use here of the adjective "crystal-clear" (or crystalline) — although he does use it of Lossky's style elsewhere.

[26] What Clément says of Evdokimov's style applies in many ways to his own. See the Introduction, pages xv–xvi, where the style of these two theologians is discussed in terms of music, Lossky being a Monteverdi to Evdokimov's Debussy.

the most advanced mathematics, as with Florensky; agricultural economy, in the case of Bulgakov; or even the death of a cat, as with Berdyaev in his old age. A religious philosopher enlightens all aspects of existence with another light. He is not a specialist, which is perhaps why specialists are only too ready to dismiss him as a poet or an adventurer of the mind. Which suits him to the ground; for he is fully alive! Berdyaev and Bulgakov, for example, had both been through Marxism and had had experience of revolutionary action and prison. Bulgakov had also been a delegate in the Duma and Berdyaev had been a member in 1917 of a short-lived pre-parliament and then, as already mentioned, became fully involved in Soviet society, being imprisoned twice by the old regime and twice by the new one before being finally expelled.

Mother Maria [Skobtsova], a former revolutionary socialist who had been married several times but who had become a nun in the emigration, travelled the length and breadth of France to help the humiliated and the aggrieved, writing poems and articles in the train. She had received permission from her bishop to preach in church. During the war she saved the lives of many Jews. When finally arrested and deported, she is believed to have taken the place of another woman on the way to the gas chambers.

None of these people were afraid of life. They were not submissive. One of them even saw in rebellion a proof of the existence of God. Together with Dostoevsky, each of them could say, "My hosanna has passed through a great crucible of doubt".[27]

---

[27] Though a similar sentence appears in *The Brothers Karamazov*, this particular formulation used by Dostoevsky of himself comes from his last notebook (1880–1).

For me, Evdokimov was a living synthesis of this religious philosophy, of the Byzantine patristic tradition, and of French thought. He said to me one day, "We Orthodox, given the historical situation of our Church, have very few possibilities to express ourselves. Nevertheless, our writings sometimes bear a distinctive mark that is hardly ever found in other Christian writings. They are not your average clerical piece of work. They bear the imperial hallmark." He was alluding to spiritual Byzantium, to its eagle. The solar, Johannine eagle.

Evdokimov's greatness was to have fully integrated into the Tradition of the undivided Church, for contemporary sharing, the occasionally exuberant and imbalanced insights of Russian religious philosophy. This was the favour he did for "sophiology", among other topics. For—despite verging on heresy—it constituted one of the most fruitful areas of research in twentieth-century Christianity. (Sometimes I dream of an "Orthodoxy"—that is, the "right glorification" of God—that would be so total that there would be no more heresies, simply concepts that were incomplete or badly contextualized. Or rather, this was the dream of Patriarch Athenagoras.)

The main representative of "sophiology" was Serge Bulgakov. He was the son of a priest. (The Christian East has retained—except for bishops—the original practice of a married clergy.) So as a child, he gained his understanding of the cosmos through the prism of the rhythm of the liturgy and the liturgical year. Later, as a Marxist theoretician, he devoted himself to agricultural problems but soon discovered that there were limits to Marxist Prometheanism. Anticipating the current concerns of ecologists, he ending by having a spiritual understanding of the earth, of matter.

Alyosha's kiss of the earth again! Thus it is no surprise that, once converted by the holiness of the earth, Bulgakov should have attempted to develop a cosmic vision of the Church. Hence his "sophiology", the doctrine of Sophia, Wisdom: the uncorrupted heart of each thing is what accounts for the sacredness of matter, its transparency to Wisdom, to the divine Light. It is a transparency that is everywhere endangered, but that is restored in the body of Christ. Since on the cross blood flowed from the pierced side of Jesus, the earth itself has become the Holy Grail! Thus the sacrament, and the Church as sacrament of the Resurrected One, are not just tacked on to the world; they are its rediscovered transparency.

It is true that Bulgakov combined all this in prolix structures—whose force is not always apparent—with a fair amount of heavy German philosophy. Yet the basic intuition of a cosmic and feminine approach to the mystery remains valid, for it was by the *fiat* of the Mother of God, "throne of Wisdom", that the created wisdom that is at the heart of things fully accepted divine Wisdom. Evdokimov kept this intuition, but founded it on the traditional teaching about God's energies. He developed it in his own reflections concerning woman and beauty. "The Holy Spirit", Father Bulgakov liked to say, "is the hypostasis of beauty."

However, I think that Paul Evdokimov was above all similar to Berdyaev, whose notion of freedom he elucidated. Creation, pinnacle of God's omnipotence, implies—and this is something, it seems to me, that Western Christianity has never dared say—both a risk on the part of the Creator and, as it were, a limit to his all-powerfulness, so that the other may have space for his freedom. Evdokimov summed up this mystery in two formulas: "God can do everything except force man to love him"; "Every great love is of necessity love crucified." He especially liked the vision of God that one finds in Nicholas Cabasilas: the ultimate proof of love is to suffer and die for those one loves, to give one's life for one's friends, as the Gospels say. But, enclosed in his own transcendence, God was unable to give us this proof of his love, and so he "invented" the totally inconceivable idea of his death on the cross, to attract to himself those who were fleeing from him in their despair and fear. This "mad love" of God for man became the very heart of Evdokimov's thought and prayer. As did the truth that it is not required of man that he should first love God, but simply that he should remember that God loves him and that he wished *to make humanity his mother* so as to become "the highest abode of human love". And also that God's silence is identical to his love, for this beggar God humbly waits at the door of our heart so that we open it in a sovereign act of freedom. Then man's heart awakens, a life vaster than his own begins to develop within him. Salvation through love—this was perhaps Evdokimov's final word, on the threshold of silence …

If we bring together the negative theology so forcefully expounded by Lossky and the theme of God's mad love that was central to Evdokimov's thinking, we have the outlines of what might be called an *apophatic antinomy*. Apophatic here refers to the ascent of the intelligence to the Inaccessible One, like Moses' ascent of Sinai. This apophatic approach is too often mistaken as being simply another way of referring to the *via negativa*; that is, an approach which rejects the possibility of any grasping of the mystery and any definition that might be a limitation. Concepts create idols of God, said one of the Fathers. It is only when left astonished that we gain a sense of something. God is beyond our images, our concepts, he is even beyond the very notion "God". He is *hypertheos*, and inaccessible. But in the face of God's mad love for us, our unknowing is changed into a deeply moving outburst of praise. It is the antinomy of the abyss and the cross that constitutes the limitless nature of this love. God's proper name is revealed in the total abandonment on the cross.

The greatness of these men was that they showed that only a deepening of liturgical and spiritual life could fertilize history. By multiplying humble but shining instances of holiness—"iconic proof", said Evdokimov, of God's existence. (A saint is of no use, but everything is enlightened in his light: "Acquire peace in the Spirit and thousands around you will be saved".[28]) By the multiplication of humble but radiant church communities in which the Eucharist becomes friendship, mutual help, a disinterested welcoming attitude of kindness and beauty. By the application to history of an ascesis of creative love. Evdokimov's pages on "inner monasticism" and the need to reduce one's needs, to free oneself, to pacify oneself—not in order to flee the world but to serve life—these pages seem prophetic today. Especially when we see so many young people wishing, via poverty, to renew a nuptial pact with the earth or else being fascinated by a Helder Camara, whose revolutionary asceticism is intensified by creative love.

These are words and examples that should not be restricted to Orthodoxy. At the heart of the West, they call all Christians to the same deepening of their faith,

---

[28] "Acquire peace in the Spirit": this is how Clément transcribes St Seraphim's famous words, though "a peaceful spirit" is more commonly found.

and invite all people to discover the youthfulness of Christianity, whilst discovering that nothing is alien to divine-humanity.

And so I discovered that Orthodoxy in France was not something confined to ethnic ghettoes or the triumphalism of fanatics. People who were already inseparably linked to the destiny of this country—admittedly being Russian in origin, though there were others who were Greek (for a sizeable emigration settled in the West after 1922 and the fall and burning of Smyrna)—accepted to be what they were without nostalgia or aggressiveness. They practised a marriage of cultures, being Orthodox here and now, unselfishly willing to share, but without breaking with their "Eastern" roots or a concrete, liturgical continuity with Orthodoxy.

These men welcomed me and I have never once felt that their friendship faltered. Their relative marginality matched my own, and at times was transfigured into the necessary marginality of a renewed Christianity that is everywhere in diaspora, everywhere crucified between exile and the kingdom.[29]

✤

At the age of thirty, I was baptized into the Orthodox Church. It was a serious but clear-headed choice, both a risk and an easy, obvious step to take. A conscious choice, if you like, though one's whole life—one's whole death!—is needed to become fully conscious of what baptismal grace really is, of what it really means to die and be born again in Christ.

---

[29] This last phrase is an allusion to the 1957 collection of six short stories by Albert Camus, of which it is the overall title. An underlying theme of these stories is feeling foreign and isolated in one's own society.

It was the first of November.[30] It was raining. It took me a long time to walk across Paris in the rain, but I wanted to accomplish this decisive pilgrimage on foot. Anyway, rain is a sign of fertility, and I was going to my own birth. Cold was the water that trickled down my face, cold and pure the baptismal water. The long series of exorcisms takes the full measure of hell and of repentance. The immersion does not last long enough to cause suffocation—more's the pity! Chrismation follows without a pause. "The gift of the seal of the Holy Spirit", says the priest as he anoints the forehead, the eyes, the ears, the nostrils, the mouth, the breast near the heart, the hands and the feet. So that from now on it is in the Spirit that one might think, see, hear, breathe, speak, act and move. It is as if the place of death had been turned upside down by the paschal cross and become a place of the Spirit. I was quite calm and displayed no excitement. Everything was beginning. Much time would be needed, I knew, for these words, these powers, this breath to shine through. But at least, from now on, the light was inside me.

I remember the Creed. Each word opens one's mind. I was told I had proclaimed it with force. I don't know. A group began to gather for the Liturgy, during which I would be the first to receive communion. Someone came up and embraced me.

---

[30] The year is 1952, as Clément specifies in *Mémoires*, 30. For the significance of 1 November in France, see page 72.

Epilogue

Many years have passed since that day when I joined the Church. She does not disappoint, once one has understood what she is: nutrient soil, a great life force offered to us. It is up to us whether or not we avail ourselves of it. As a child, I wanted to live close to the sea. To console me, my grandfather would hold a shell to my ear and get me to hear the sound of the waves. The Church is the sea that sings for ever in the shell of the world.

I have lost the naive and somewhat blinkered attitude of the recent convert. I have taken stock of the historical weakness of Orthodoxy, also of its tenacious patience and, in many places, its fruitful passion. I have observed the modesty, the temptation to withdraw into itself, and yet the reality, of the Orthodox presence in western Europe. I too have become more than modest. But I walk close to the sea.

In the azure-blue of the sky is emblazoned for me now a face—the Face of the crucified Pantocrator, the transfigured Man of Sorrows. One day in Greece, bathed in a light even more intense than that of my childhood, I entered the freshness of a church. The blue of the cupola represented the full benediction of the sky, but a face was depicted on it. Going into this church was like a summing up of my entire journey: from an azure sky that was empty to one that was full;

from a blue sky enclosed in its own beauty, but with darkness beyond, to one that radiates around the Face of faces, with love filling all that is beyond. From light to another light.

A light that not only glows in one's heart, but that shines in every face.

From now on, I need no longer speak about myself. I wanted to tell of an encounter. Faith is a new beginning. One should not toy with it—whether to have it or not. One ought to go down into that crypt—both ecclesial and personal—where living water springs forth, and then emerge again ready to share everything. "He shall go in and go out and shall find pasture."[1] My life no longer belongs to me, it is that of a useless servant. In any situation, what I try to do or say focuses on how to discern my part in it and that of others. All grows from that friendship which begins to understand, however little, the inexhaustible impartiality with which God gives himself to sinners and publicans.

I do not consider Orthodoxy to be one more denomination alongside others. What I love and revere about her is her faithfulness to the Origin and the End of Christianity: that Christ-like divine-humanity in which the Spirit breathes. It is a stubborn faithfulness, but one that is inspired by the Spirit, and intelligent. Half-buried under a hostile history, it is "the pillar and ground of the truth",[2] a Truth that transforms and revitalizes intelligence—all aspects of human intelligence, which is something that so many Christians today seem to fear and prefer to ignore. Yes, I think of Orthodoxy as a foundation, as solid ground, as roots, as a crypt. And also as an End, as universal transfiguration.

[1] Jn 10:9.
[2] 1 Tim 3:15.

What is needed is a mutually enriching encounter between the Eastern sense of mystery and the Western sense of historical responsibility. Orthodoxy reminds the West that though God was crucified, man was deified. The Christian West reminds Orthodoxy that one cannot say without doing. Such an encounter would sketch out the new face of a divine-humanity.

Occasionally, with a touch of irony, I think to myself that in becoming Orthodox I was striving to reconcile my various ancestors—Catholic, Protestant and socialist. When Lorenzatos spoke of a lost centre, he had in mind the high poetry of the West; as for me, I have been using the phrase in connection with those country folk.[3] I can no longer judge from the outside the destiny—now become global—of Western Christianity: Rome, the Reformation, the sacrament of the brother. For, despite appearances, Orthodoxy has in effect become for Western Christianity no longer something external, but internal. I try ... we try, to stammer out a word of unity on behalf of all. We Orthodox in the West are like seeds who should neither impose ourselves nor isolate ourselves, but rather bury ourselves in this earth, in this history where God has sown us. To die and, if God wills, to be born again, joining others in fostering every germ of unity, and all movements of renewal. What this resurrection will be, what form

[3] In his essay (written in 1961) Lorenzatos argues that serious Western poetry has progressively lost its spiritual centre, its metaphysical vision, tending at best to focus on aesthetics. His writings have never been taken up by any French publisher, but this particular essay was translated by Olivier Clément's friend Jacques Tourraille. It was accepted by Clément for inclusion in *Contacts* and appeared in print in 1976. This explains why it was fresh in his mind when composing this spiritual autobiography (dated 1975); he references it on the first page and returns to it here, towards its close.

it will take, is not for us to decide. Yet sometimes—for example, with the Dominicans at Toulouse, at Eygalières, at Aubazine or at Poligny—I believe I already see re-emerging the undivided Church, and I hope and know that the Orthodox presence in this land counts for something.[4] In the Cévennes where my mother's family came from, a few monks, disciples of Father Sophrony, often come to pray in an isolated village where a poor couple have settled. The husband, who has spent time on Patmos with a hermit and became Orthodox there, is now entirely devoted to the translation of the liturgical and spiritual texts of Orthodoxy.[5]

As you come down from the Causse du Larzac plateau to the mountains that are scorched and full of terrifying ravines—it is not yet the greener Cévennes, but pitiless limestone rock looking like a gigantic pile of bones—there is one of those deserted hamlets that strangely encircle my village. One of my aunts was its school teacher, at a time when a few families still lived there. Later she killed herself. So it was with astonishment that I read André Miquel's fine novel whose title is taken from the name of this hamlet: *Les Lavagnes*.[6]

[4] Since 1965, a Greek Melkite community has given a new lease of life to the twelfth-century Cistercian abbey in Aubazine. Dominican André Gouzes has composed liturgical music which is heavily influenced by Russian chant and is widely used, not just in Toulouse and not just by Dominicans. Moreover, since 1975 when *L'Autre Soleil* was first published, the influence of Orthodoxy—with regard to iconography, the rite or the music—has grown exponentially in France.

[5] The person in question is Jacques Touraille. Cf. note 3.

[6] The novel was published in 1973, shortly before Clément's spiritual autobiography came out. The hamlet—whose name is a transliteration of the Occitan for a dew pond—is but a couple of kilometres as the crow flies from Saint-Guilhelm-le-Désert (and Olivier Clément's's birthplace, Aniane). See page 85, note 11.

It is the tragic story, ending in suicide, of the teacher sent to this place where woven together are burning heat, madness and a kind of solar death. Not far away is an ancient hermitage that I have often climbed up to. From the rock face that curves over the chapel oozes water, at once eerie and promising in this desert of a spot. For centuries, the hermitage was abandoned—a dead place in a land of death. But in the last few years it has been reopened. The hermit is Catholic but follows the Byzantine rite. He is sustained by the philokalic tradition, invoking the divine-human Name. It is a difficult vocation, still fragile. Yet for me it is a deeply moving sign.

"In thy light shall we see light."

Come, Paraclete, Spirit of Truth, "who art in all places and fillest all things".[7]

---

[7] From the prayer, "O Heavenly King", which introduces every public Orthodox service, as well as private Morning and Evening Prayers

Bibliography

In this non-exhaustive list of books, titles are in order of publication. Avalilable English translations are given in brackets.

Transfigurer le temps: Notes sur le temps à la lumière de la tradition orthodoxe. Paris: Delachaux & Niestlé, 1959. (*Transfiguring Time: Understanding Time in the Light of the Orthodox Tradition,* trans. Jeremy N. Ingpen. New York: New City Press, 2019.)

Qu'est-ce que l'Église orthodoxe? Périgueux: Centre œcuménique Enotikon, 1961. (*The Church of Orthodoxy.* New York: Chelsea House Publications, 2001.)

L'Église orthodoxe. Collection "Que sais-je?" Paris: Presses Universitaires de France, 1961. Multiple editions since. Little known in the English-speaking world, this is probably his most widely distributed book.

L'Essor du christianisme oriental. Paris: Presses Universitaires de France, 1964; Desclée de Brouwer, 2009.

Byzance et le christianisme. Paris: Presses Universitaires de France, 1964; Desclée de Brouwer, 2010.

"Dionysos et le ressuscité: Essai de réponse chrétienne à l'athéisme contemporain" (with Jean Bosc and M. J. Le Guillou) in *Évangile et révolution,* pp. 65–122. Paris: Centurion, 1968.

Dialogues avec le Patriarche Athénagoras. Paris: Fayard, 1969; 2nd enlarged edition 1976.

Questions sur l'homme. Paris: Stock, 1972; Québec: Éditions Anne Sigier, 1986. (*On Human Being: A Spiritual Anthropology,* trans. Jeremy Hummerstone. London: New City Press, 2000.)

L'Esprit de Soljenitsyne. Paris: Stock, 1974. (*The Spirit of Solzhenitsyn*, trans. P. Burns and S. Fawcett. London: Search Press; New York: Barnes & Noble, 1976.)

La Liberté du Christ (avec Guy Riobé). Paris: Stock/Cerf, 1974.

La Douloureuse Joie: Aperçus sur la prière personnelle de l'Orient chrétien (with Élisabeth Behr-Sigel, Boris Bobrinskoy and M. Lot-Borodine). Bégrolles-en-Mauges: Abbaye de Bellefontaine, 1974.

L'Autre Soleil: Quelques notes d'autobiographie spirituelle. Paris: Stock, 1975; Desclée de Brouwer, 2008. (*The Other Sun: A Spiritual Autobiography*, trans. Michael Donley. Leominster: Gracewing, 2021.)

Le Christ, Terre des vivants: Essais théologiques. Bégrolles-en-Mauges: Abbaye de Bellefontaine, 1975.

Le Mystère pascal: Commentaires liturgiques (with Alexander Schmemann). Bégrolles-en-Mauges: Abbaye de Bellefontaine, 1975.

La Prière du cœur (with Jacques Serr). Bégrolles-en-Mauges: Abbaye de Bellefontaine, 1977. Clément's contribution constitutes the second part of the book: pp. 43–98.

Le Visage intérieur. Paris: Stock, 1978; Salvator, 2017.

La Révolte de l'Esprit: Repères pour la situation spirituelle d'aujourd'hui. (Interviews with Stanislas Rougier). Paris: Stock, 1979.

Sources: Les mystiques chrétiens des origines. Paris: Stock, 1982; Desclée de Brouwer, 2008. (*The Roots of Christian Mysticism*, trans. T. Berkeley and J. Hummerstone. London: New City Press, 1993; 2nd edn 2013.)

Le Chant des larmes: Essai sur le repentir. Suivi de la traduction du Grand Canon par saint André de Crète. Paris: Desclée de Brouwer, 1982; 2011. (*The Song of Tears: An Essay on Repentance based on the Great Canon of St Andrew of Crete*, trans. Michael Donley. Yonkers, NY: St Vladimir's Seminary Press, 2021.)

Orient–Occident. Deux passeurs: Vladimir Lossky et Paul Evdokimov. Geneva: Labor et Fides, 1985.

Les Visionnaires: Essai sur le dépassement du nihilisme. Paris: Desclée de Brouwer, 1986.

Un respect têtu: Islam et Christianisme (with Mohamed Talbi). Paris: Nouvelle Cité, 1989.
Anachroniques. Paris: Desclée de Brouwer, 1990.
Berdiaev: un philosophe russe en France. Paris: Desclée de Brouwer, 1991.
Rome autrement: Une réflexion orthodoxe sur la papauté. Paris: Desclée de Brouwer, 1992. (*You are Peter: An Orthodox Theologian's Reflection on the Exercise of Papal Primacy*, trans. M. S. Laird. London & New York: New City Press, 2003.)
Trois prières: Le Notre Père, la prière au Saint Esprit, la prière de saint Ephrem. Paris: Desclée de Brouwer, 1993. Also included in the 2011 reprint of *Le Chant des larmes*. (*Three Prayers: The Lord's Prayer, O Heavenly King, the Prayer of St Ephrem*, trans. M. Breck. Yonkers, NY: St Vladimir's Seminary Press, 2000.
"*Le Christ du credo*" in *Le Christianisme* (with J. Baubérot and J. Rogues). Paris: Fayard, 1993. Clément's long chapter constitutes the first third of the book, the remainder being the contributions of a Roman Catholic and a Protestant.
L'Œil de feu: Deux visions spirituelles du cosmos. Fontfroide-le-Haut: Fata Morgana, 1994; Clichy: Éditions de Corlevour, 2013.
Corps de mort et de gloire: Petite introduction à une théopoétique du corps. Paris: Desclée de Brouwer, 1995.
"*Introduction à la spiritualité philocalique*" in *La Philocalie des Pères neptiques* (trad. Jacques Touraille), vol. 1, pp. 7–33. Paris: Desclée de Brouwer/ J.-C. Lattès, 1995.
La Vérité vous rendra libre: Entretiens avec le patriarche œcuménique Bartholomée 1ᵉʳ. Paris: Desclée de Brouwer; J.- C. Lattès, 1996. (*Conversations with Ecumenical Patriarch Bartholomew I*, trans. Paul Meyendorff. Crestwood, NY: St Vladimir's Seminary Press, 1997.)
Taizé: Un sens à la vie. Paris: Bayard; Centurion, 1997. (*Taizé: A Meaning to Life*. Chicago: GIA Publications, 1997.)
Les Quatres Évangiles: Présentées et annotées par Olivier Clément. Paris: Gallimard, 1998.
Le Chemin de Croix à Rome. Paris: Desclée de Brouwer, 1998.

Déracine-toi et plante-toi dans la mer. Québec: Éditions Anne Sigier, 1998.

Le Christ est ressuscité: propos sur les fêtes chrétiennes. Paris: Desclée de Brouwer, 2000.

Sillons de lumière. Troyes: Fates; Paris: Cerf, 2002.

Mémoires d'espérance: Entretiens avec Jean-Claude Noyer. Paris: Desclée de Brouwer, 2003.

Espace infini de liberté: Le Saint Esprit et Marie Théotokos. Québec: Éditions Anne Sigier, 2005.

Le Pélerin immobile. Québec: Éditions Anne Sigier, 2006.

Petite Boussole spirituelle pour notre temps. Paris: Desclée de Brouwer, 2008.

Une saison en littérature, ed. F. Damour. Paris: Desclée de Brouwer, 2013.

Joie de la Résurrection, ed. F. Damour. Paris: Salvator, 2015.

CPSIA information can be obtained
at www.ICGtesting.com
Printed in the USA
LVHW031126060521
686680LV00008B/259